Sex, gender, and Sexual Behavior

Chapter Outline

FREEZE FRAME

In 1965, twin boys were born to Janet and Ron Reimer. In a freak accident, the penis of one of the twins, Bruce, was so badly burned that it literally fell off after several days. The medical team offered to attempt reconstructive surgery, but the chances of success were small. While they were weighing the possibility of surgery, the Reimers happened to see a controversial but respected sex researcher named John Money on a television program. Dr. Money had recently coined the term *gender identity* to refer to a person's inner sense of being male or female, and he expressed the view—unsubstantiated by scientific evidence—that the genetic sex of an individual was not a critical factor in determining the person's gender identity. The critical factor, according to Money, was socialization—how the person was reared by parents and viewed by society. Ultimately, this view was to assume the status of gospel in the profession. More important, Money was a pioneer in procedures known as sex reassignment surgery that could allow a person to alter his or her genital sex if desired.

The Reimers consulted Money, and he suggested sex reassignment for Bruce. Surgery was performed to create external female genitals, the child was renamed Brenda, and she was reared as a girl—without ever being told of her birth history. Following the surgery, Janet and Ron Reimer struggled hard to enforce gender differences between Brenda and her brother Brian. Brian was allowed to shave with his father, whereas Brenda was made to play with makeup and wear dresses. She was given dolls and told to be neat and tidy.

However, these efforts appeared to be in vain. There was nothing feminine about Brenda. By age 2 she was angrily tearing off her dresses. She refused to play with her dolls, and would repeatedly steal her brother's toy cars and guns, beating him up for good measure. She acted like a boy in the way she spoke, sat, moved, and played. As Brenda's teachers reported, she simply seemed to be a boy "by nature."

When she turned 10, Brenda began to exhibit sexual attraction to girls, and at age 11 the pubertal changes associated with being a boy kicked in—including increased muscle mass in the upper torso and lowered vocal frequency. She was ridiculed at school and given the name "Cavewoman." Her school life deteriorated. Compelled to undergo hormonal therapy by Money and by her parents, she started to develop breasts and fat deposits around her hips as a result of the injections—but she used overeating and weight gain as a strategy to try to hide this feminization of her figure.

Bruce/Brenda's case was unveiled to the world by Money in a 1972 book in which Brenda's obvious lack of adaptation to life as a female was strangely mischaracterized, perhaps to make it appear that Money's theory and strategy were correct. But the book had wide appeal because it fit well with the zeitgeist, or social climate, of the time—when many activists were struggling against sexism and sought to assert the idea that there were no biological bases for sex differences. Money's version of Brenda Reimer's story found its way into textbooks on psychology, sociology, child development, and human sexuality. This version strongly influenced the way people thought about sex and gender.

But the family's troubles were escalating. Brenda dropped out of school, and her mother was admitted to a psychiatric ward to prevent suicidal behavior. Her father was drinking heavily. Brenda's psychiatrist decided it was time for Brenda's parents to tell her the truth. In a highly emotional conversation, Brenda's father tearfully told Brenda the facts, step by step. Brenda reported that she felt anger, amazement, and disbelief. But, above all, "I was relieved. Suddenly it all made sense why I felt the way I did. I wasn't some sort of weirdo. I wasn't crazy" (Colapinto, 2000, p. 180).

Brenda Reimer changed her name to David, began life as a boy, and after a seemingly endless series of painful surgeries successfully grew into a fairly handsome man who ultimately married and raised a step-family for many years—until his life took a downward turn, and he committed suicide in May of 2004.

This story is compelling and tragic. But the details of David Reimer's life, originally published by medical sex researcher Milton Diamond and psychiatrist Keith Sigmundson (1999) and later elaborated upon by journalist John Colapinto (2000), raise a great many questions: What is sex? What is gender? To what extent do our genes, genitals, hormones, societies, and cultures shape the way we see ourselves and others see us as sexual beings? How do they influence sexual behavior?

It might be tempting to conclude from the details of David Reimer's life that biological factors such as genes and hormones are primarily responsible for whether we see ourselves as male or female, and whether we are attracted to men or women as sexual partners. However, as emphasized in the first chapter of this book, drawing general conclusions from one case study or anecdote is a dangerous endeavor. And, as it turns out, the issue is even more complicated than the story of Bruce/Brenda/David might indicate. This is demonstrated in long-term studies of dozens of genetic males who were raised as females because they had been born with various rare conditions which prohibited them from developing normal male genitals. As would be expected on the basis of David Reimer's story, these studies do show that as many as two-thirds of these individuals never adjusted, and ultimately identified as men. However, a substantial number *did* adjust and continued to identify themselves as female (Cohen-Kettenis, 2005; Meyer-Bahlburg, 2005). Thus, genes and hormones cannot fully account for how we come to view ourselves as male or female.

Sex, gender, and sexual behavior are all captured under the umbrella label **human sexuality**. The psychology of human sexuality is the topic of this chapter.

Human sexuality ▶ An umbrella label describing human sex, gender, and sexual behavior.

Are "Sex" and "Gender" Different?

Two or three hundred years ago, the term *sex* was understood to refer to the state of being either male or female. Sex applied equally to all animals, including humans. Sex was not something you could *have*, in those days—it was something you *belonged to* or *were*. Beginning a little more than 100 years ago, the meaning of the term *sex* began to broaden so that it came to refer to sexual behavior as well as sexual anatomy. Sex now became something a person could *have*, although sharp differences of opinion continue to exist about whether or not one is actually "having it" at any given time (as discussed later in this chapter).

Over the past few decades, the term *gender* has been introduced into the fray to complicate things even more. Before tackling the often tricky distinctions between *sex* and *gender*, let us first clarify what is meant by the term "sex," as in *male* and *female*.

Sex at Birth Is Chromosomal, Gonadal, Hormonal, and Anatomical

As attested by birthing room exclamations upon a baby's emergence into the world—"It's a girl!" / "It's a boy!"—the sex to which a person belongs is almost always immediately obvious. However, it is not *always* obvious, even after careful scrutiny of the evidence. For example, controversies have arisen during the Olympic games over whether certain female athletes ought to be considered "female" (Mealey, 2000). Actually, the sex of a human being at birth is determined by four characteristics: *chromosomes, the fetal gonad, the hormonal balance of the fetus*, and *genitals*. (Table 16.1 summarizes the four factors.)

CHROMOSOMAL SEX

The first determinant of sex is *chromosomal*, or genetic. Recall from Chapter 3 that the inner kernel of each human cell (except the reproductive cell) contains 23 pairs of chromosomes, the rod-like bodies which house human DNA. One pair of the set of 23 is the *sex chromosome* pair. The female sex chromosome is known as an X-chromosome, and the male, the Y-chromosome. Each

Table 16.1 Four Factors Determine Sex at Birth

Unless a fetus is intersex, the following sequence of factors determines sex at birth.

FACTOR	DESCRIPTION
Chromosomal (genetic) sex	A female infant (XX) has inherited one X chromosome from each parent; a male infant (XY) has inherited one X chromosome from his mother and one Y chromosome from his father.
Fetal gonads (reproductive organs)	The gonads produce either male or female reproductive cells (gametes). The female gonads are the ovaries; the male gonads are the testes. Gonads begin to develop at about 7 weeks for males, 9 weeks for females.
Hormonal balance of the fetus	If the fetus is male in chromosomal and gonadal sex, the testes' production of testosterone and Mullerian inhibiting substance (MIS) lead to the development of male genitals; if the fetus is female, production of these hormones is not triggered, and female genitals develop.
Anatomical sex (sexual organs, or genitals)	Genitals (vulva/vagina or penis) develop as a consequence of the hormonal balance of the fetus. Development of genitals is complete by about 16 weeks.

person inherits one sex chromosome from the mother and one from the father, making up the pair of sex chromosomes. To be born female, you must inherit two X chromosomes, so females are referred to as XX. Males inherit one X and one Y chromosome, so they are referred to as XY.

However, females, being XX, only possess X chromosomes, and therefore can only pass on an X chromosome to their offspring. At the chromosomal level, whether an embryo is male or female is therefore entirely determined by whether the fertilizing sperm cell carries with it a Y or an X chromosome.

THE FETAL GONADS

The second determinant of sex is the fetal **gonads**, or reproductive organs. In the male, the gonads are the **testes**. In the female, they are the **ovaries**. The gonads produce either male or female reproductive cells, known as *gametes*. Until about the seventh week of gestation, there are no fetal gonads—the human embryo only possesses chromosomal sex, and its internal sexual organs have not yet developed in either a male or female direction.

At about 7 weeks, if the sperm that fertilized the mother's ovum bore the Y chromosome, a single "master" gene, known as the SRY, triggers a complex of genes which create the proteins that develop into the male gonads, the testes. If this complex of genes is not triggered by about 9 weeks—because the sperm bore an X chromosome and the SRY is therefore not present—the embryo develops ovaries, the female gonads. Except under rare circumstances, by the end of this process the embryo is either male or female.

HORMONAL BALANCE OF THE FETUS

The third determinant of sex is the *hormonal balance of the fetus*. Contrary to popular belief, hormones such as *estrogen* and *testosterone* are manufactured in both male and female bodies. However, the *balance* among the hormones differs from male to female. Male bodies produce more testosterone (primarily in the testes) and female bodies produce more estrogen (primarily in the ovaries). In male fetuses, the testes' production of testosterone and another hormone, known as the *Mullerian inhibiting substance (MIS)*, leads to the development of the male genitals and the suppression of female genital development. If this hormonal bath is not triggered, due to the absence of testes, female genitals will develop. Thus, the human embryo is essentially "poised" to develop as a female, and will only become male in the presence of testosterone

Gonads ▶ Reproductive organs which produce reproductive cells, or *gametes*. The male gonad is the testes; the female gonad is the ovaries.

Testes ▶ The male gonad.

Ovaries ▶ The female gonad.

and MIS—just as a genetically male embryo can only develop if the fertilizing sperm bears a Y-chromosome.

ANATOMICAL SEX

The fourth determinant of sex is the actual development of male or female **genitals**, or sexual organs, as a consequence of the hormonal balance of the fetus. The male sexual organ is the *penis*, and the female sexual organs are the *vulva* (including the *clitoris*) and the *vagina*. Sexual organs differ from reproductive organs (ovaries, testes) in that sexual organs serve nonreproductive as well as reproductive functions. Development of genitals is completed approximately 16 weeks after fertilization.

In the vast majority of cases these four factors—chromosomes, fetal gonads, hormonal balance, and anatomy—coincide to produce infants who are unambiguously male or female. If female chromosomes are in place for the embryo, then female hormonal balance, female gonads, and female genitals will nearly always also develop; similarly, male chromosomes nearly always coincide with male hormonal balance, gonads, and genitals. However, there are unusual exceptions known as *intersex*. In these cases, the either/or categories *male* and *female* do not apply, or they apply to a lesser degree. Specifically, the term **intersex** refers to a number of conditions where:

- As a result of genetic abnormality, a male (XY) infant is born with the appearance of female genitals, or a female (XX) infant is born with the appearance of male genitals;

or

- An infant is born with aspects of both male *and* female gonads and genital tissue, a condition termed *gonadal intersexuality* (referred to in the past as *hermaphroditism*). Gonadal intersexes, like the majority of intersexes, are infertile and unable to bear children (Sytsma, 2007).

Although rare,[1] intersex is important because it demonstrates that the two-sex system, the rule among mammalian and most other forms of life, is not at all inevitable. (It also sets the stage for our discussion of *transgender* later in this chapter.)

"Gender" Is Less Easy to Define than "Sex"

As you can see, sex is multifaceted. However, it is also relatively easy to define in scientific terms. *Gender* is not so easy to pin down. During the 1950s, John Money (the same John Money discussed in the "Freeze Frame" feature which opened this chapter) began to use the word *gender* as part of the term **gender identity**—our subjective perception of the sex to which we belong or with which we identify. During the late 1970s, use of the term *gender* was greatly broadened to promote the idea that what were then termed *sex roles* (beliefs about appropriate male and female behavior) and *sex differences* were in fact social and psychological categories—not part of human biology and therefore not inevitable. Researchers such as Rhoda Unger proposed that

Genitals ▶ Male and female sexual organs. Although sexual organs may serve reproductive functions, they serve functions related to sexual behavior and elimination of urine as well. The male sexual organ is the penis; the female sexual organs are the vulva (including the clitoris) and the vagina.

Intersex ▶ Unusual genetic, anatomical, or neurohormonal conditions which render it difficult to classify an infant as strictly male or female.

Gender identity ▶ Each person's subjective perception of the sex to which he or she belongs and/or with which he or she identifies. Gender identity develops in early childhood as a consequence of genetic, hormonal, and social factors.

---

[1]*Because the idea of intersex as "rare" has been contested by some intersex advocates and researchers (e.g., Fausto-Sterling, 2000), I am defining "rare" here according to the standards set by the Rare Disease Act of 2002 (RDA). Although intersex is* not *a disease—it is a condition or event—according to the RDA,* rare *represents a condition experienced by fewer than 200,000 individuals. If defined in strict terms, intersex occurs in approximately 1 out of every 10,000 births in the United States (Sax, 2002), and therefore affects only 50,000 Americans. However, Fausto-Sterling and the Intersex Society of North America (www .isna.org) include conditions in their definitions of intersex not considered to be true intersex under the stricter definition. From this perspective, intersex is no longer rare and occurs in about 1 out of 2,000 births, affecting about 1,500,000 Americans.*

Gender ▶ The term originally applied to human beings during the 1960s as part of *gender identity* and later broadened to refer to all aspects of maleness and femaleness that were assumed to be primarily psychological or social in nature, rather than biological.

only anatomical sex characteristics should be described by the term *sex*, and all "non-biological" characteristics—social or psychological characteristics—should be described with the term **gender** (Unger, 1979). To use the terms *gender role* and *gender difference* in place of *sex role* and *sex difference*, for example, came to imply that the person who spoke or wrote in this way did not consider such differences to be biologically innate and therefore inevitable (e.g., Caplan & Caplan, 2005).

Because theorists favoring this approach were quite influential, over the last few decades of the 20th century the term *gender* came to replace the term *sex* altogether in a great many contexts in discussions of human behavior, although use of the term *gender* has always been inconsistent (Halpern, 2004). These changes in terminology were part of a movement toward civil rights for women and sexual minorities which flowered during the late 1960s and early 1970s. Introduction of the term *gender* also allowed for a broadening of the way people came to think about their own "maleness" and "femaleness."

However, the reader who has come this far in the book may detect two problems with the practice of separating *sex* and *gender*. First, *biological* is not synonymous with *inevitable* or *innate*, nor is *social* or *psychological* synonymous with *flexible* or *changeable* (Beck, 2010; Greenberg & Bailey, 1994). For example, numerous characteristics or tendencies with which a person is born ("biological" and likely "innate" characteristics) are vastly easier to change—through willpower, medication, meditation, legislation, therapy, exercise, surgery, and numerous other methods—than are many "psychological" characteristics and habits that a person acquires over time (learns), and which resist virtually all efforts at change (Greenberg & Bailey, 1994).

A good case in point is *paraphilia*—sexual interests that are unusual, inflexible, and which sometimes may cause problems for the person who has them or for others—for example, *pedophilia* (sexual interest in children below the age of puberty), *fetishism* (sexual interest in various inanimate objects), or *voyeurism* (sexual interest in observing people without their knowledge as they undress, have sex, or engage in other intimate behaviors). Paraphilias are not "innate" in the sense that one does not come into the world with a paraphilia in place—they are acquired over time, usually in adolescence or young adulthood. Yet paraphilias are extraordinarily resistant to change, and treatments are quite often unsuccessful. Thus, simply labeling something "social" or "psychological" in no way implies that it is more flexible or easier to change than something "biological" or "innate."

More important, dividing psychological phenomena into categories of "biological" and "not-biological" expresses a way of looking at human life that is misleading. As we have seen numerous times over the course of this book, relatively few researchers continue to adhere to a "nature vs. nurture" model of human behavior. Most support some type of model that acknowledges the interactions of biology, society, and psychology. In Diane Halpern's words, "biology and environment are as inseparable as conjoined twins who share a common heart" (2004, p. 138). Thus, increasing numbers of researchers, including many who very strongly support feminist and egalitarian ideals (e.g., Severin & Wyer, 2000), have come to believe that separating *sex* and *gender* may cause more confusion than it cures. These researchers propose that the practice may have outlived its usefulness (Halpern et al., 2007).

The reader will note that I have adopted Diane Halpern and colleagues' (2007) practice of using the term *sex* in most cases in this book, unless referring to phenomena or situations that unambiguously call for use of the term *gender*—for example, in discussions of *gender identity*, *transgender*, or other concepts whose names are solidly wedded to their meanings; or when necessary to avoid confusion between "sex" as in sexual behavior and "sex" as in male and female. Occasionally, the amalgam *sex/gender* seems the best choice. If these decisions appear inconsistent or otherwise unsatisfying, I apologize, but please take my word that it is not currently possible to write broadly about men and women without a certain amount of inconsistency in use of the terms *sex* and *gender* (Severin & Wyer, 2000).

To sum up: All human behavior has biological, psychological, and social causes and contexts. Characteristics resulting from "biological" causes are not necessarily more difficult to change than those resulting from "social" or "psychological" causes. Use of the term *sex* does not imply that the difference or attribute being discussed is inevitable and not subject to change, just as use of the term *gender* does not imply that the difference or attribute is easily changed, or even possible to change.

Gender Identity Begins in Early Childhood

As mentioned earlier, *gender identity* is a person's subjective sense of the sex to which he or she belongs. Gender identity is a fundamental dimension along which human beings organize the world (Bigler, 1997). It is an intrinsic part of each person's sense of self—the awareness of his or her own individual nature, characteristics, and very existence (Ruscher & Hammer, 2004).

When does gender identity begin to form? Boys and girls (especially girls) begin to understand the idea of gender as expressed in labels ("lady," "man") at about 17 or 18 months, and beginning in the third year (between 24 and 30 months) most children show fairly consistent awareness of their own sex or gender (A. Campbell, Shirley, Heywood, & Crook, 2000; Martin & Ruble, 2009; Renk, Donnelly, McKinney, & Agliata, 2006; Zosuls et al., 2009). If children begin to recognize their own sex/gender in the third year, exactly *how* does this developmental process occur?

One interesting approach to this question is known as **gender schema theory**, a cognitive theory of gender development (Martin & Ruble, 2004, 2009; Martin, Ruble, & Szkrybalo, 2002). A *gender schema* is a cognitive model—a template in the child's mind—about gender. According to this theory, over time, young toddlers come to acquire ideas about gender that they actively form into schemas. The schema summarizes the child's interpretations of all the information he or she has acquired about gender—for example, that there are two sexes, male and female, that she is a girl, that Mommy is a woman and Daddy is a man, that boys are dorky and like to have burping contests, and so forth.

Once acquired, this schema controls the way the toddler attends to, responds to, and recalls information about gender-related aspects of his or her environment. For example, if "boys are dorky" becomes part of a little girl's gender schema, she might recall more instances of boys' dorky behavior, while recalling fewer instances of their nondorky behavior. This strengthens her gender schema about boys.

As toddlers learn to categorize people and animals in terms of their sex/gender, this information becomes part of the schema they draw upon as they develop an understanding of their own "gender-of-self." The toddler may then attempt to behave in ways that are associated with her gender-of-self schema (e.g., "Girls play more quietly than boys. I'm a girl, so I'll play more quietly than my brother."). In a sense, the child is socializing herself in regard to her gender (Martin & Ruble, 2009).

Although gender schema theory provides one reasonable framework for understanding how gender identity develops, it is incomplete. It provides an explanation for *how* gender identity develops over time, but it does not explain *why* this process begins in the first place. If you recall from the discussion of sex differences in aggression in Chapter 10, it is a *proximate* rather than *ultimate* explanation for the development of gender identity. Although toddlers may come to view themselves as male or female as the result of gender schemas, *why* do they develop a gender schema at all? What makes sex/gender so important?

Evolutionary theorists such as Anne Campbell propose that an infant's own sex, and the sex of important adults and other children around her, have

Gender schema theory ▶ A cognitive theory of gender development which describes the way each child forms a mental template about gender which changes over time as a result of social experiences.

▲ **Gender Identity: A Fundamental Dimension of Self.** Gender identity generally does not develop until well into the third year of life. According to gender schema theory, small children actively construct gender schemas based upon their interpretations of the gender-related information they have acquired. Evolutionary theorists suggest that tacit, or preverbal, knowledge of gender is a human psychological adaptation—"primed" to develop before children can put verbal labels to their understanding of gender.

Transsexual ▶ A person who identifies with the sex other than the one to which he or she was assigned at birth and takes at least some steps to present himself or herself as a person of that other sex.

Sex reassignment surgery ▶ A surgical procedure sometimes chosen by transsexuals where artificial genitals of the sex with which the transsexual identifies are formed from his or her own genital tissue as well as inorganic (plastic) material.

always comprised information that has been highly relevant to the struggle to survive. Consequently human beings may have evolved a tacit, or *preverbal*, level of understanding of gender that develops much earlier than the third year—before the infant is able to affix a verbal label to this understanding (A. Campbell et al., 2000). Mechanisms such as gender schemas may then explain how gender identity develops and grows further in early childhood. In this way, evolutionary theory contributes a (speculative) *why* to complement the (speculative) *how* of gender schema and similar theories which focus on the child's experiences in the world during early development (e.g., Bussey & Bandura, 1999).

GENDER IDENTITY IS NOT LIMITED TO "MALE" AND "FEMALE"

As suggested in the brief discussion of intersex on p. 775, gender identity may sometimes include more numerous categories than "male" and "female." For example, the term **transsexual** describes a person who identifies with the sex other than the one to which he or she was assigned at birth, and ultimately takes at least some steps to present himself or herself as a person of that other sex. Unlike intersex—where a person's genetic sex is mismatched to his or her anatomical sex—transsexuals experience a mismatch between their anatomical sex and their *gender identity*. Some transsexuals decide to receive **sex reassignment surgery**, where their birth sex genitals are removed and artificial genitals of the sex to which they are transitioning are surgically constructed; while others are content to receive *sex reassignment therapy*—hormonal treatments to change their body shape, while keeping the genitals with which they were born. The process of altering one's body through surgery or therapy to resemble a person of the other sex is known as *transitioning*.

Transsexuals are a subset of a larger umbrella category known as **transgender**, sometimes also termed *gender identity variants* (Meyer-Bahlburg, 2010). Transgender can refer to any and all situations where a person is unhappy with the gender to which he or she was assigned at birth. This includes transsexuals, who specifically identify with the other sex and take steps to live as a member of that sex. But it also includes any type of "gender bending," including *cross-dressers* (people who dress as the other sex but retain their identification with their own sex); individuals who consider themselves to be both male *and* female (*androgynous*), or *neither* male nor female (a third gender); and those who consider the transgression of gender norms to be a political act, erotically interesting, or merely fun to do. Transgenders may also have any type of sexual orientation—they may be *straight, gay* or *lesbian, bisexual, pansexual* (attracted to every sex and gender), or *asexual* (not interested in sex at all). The point is that *transgender* is really a term of identity, to be adopted or rejected as each person chooses. It is not a technical or scientific designation (Israel & Tarver, 2001).

It also should be said that terminology, definitions, and other aspects of transgender and intersex are quite controversial and in flux. Opinions about proper terminology and about the very meaning of transgender and intersex can give rise to heated arguments (Meyer-Bahlburg, 2010). This is because conflicts often exist between the perspectives, beliefs, and aspirations of the transgendered and intersexed themselves, and those of researchers and clinicians who may study them or come into contact with them.

Gender Roles Are Beliefs about How Men and Women Ought to Behave

Lia is the exceptionally bright daughter of one of my colleagues. When Lia was 8, she dragged her mother to see *Spider-Man 2* at the local multiplex. As they waited in line, Lia noticed that those waiting to see *Spider-Man 2* were almost all boys, while those waiting to see *Chronicles of Narnia* were almost all girls.

▲ **Transgender Means Different Things to Different People.** *Transgender* is a term of identity that can refer to any and all situations where a person is unhappy in the gender to which he or she was assigned at birth. Transgenders may be straight, gay, lesbian, bisexual, pansexual (interested in all sexes and genders), or asexual (uninterested in sex). Transgender may also be seen as a political act or something fun to do.

▲ **Gender Roles Are Acquired in Childhood.** Although gender roles may differ to some degree from culture to culture, in many respects they are also remarkably similar across cultures. Gender roles are acquired in childhood and refined over time. Children pick and choose from the cultural "menu" of gender-related behaviors offered them.

After a few moments of uneasy fidgeting, she turned to her mother and asked, "Can we see the Narnia movie instead?" Startled, her mother asked her why she had changed her mind so quickly. Lia mumbled, "Oh, *Spider-Man*'s for boys. . . ."

At age 8 (somewhat to her mother's dismay), Lia was an extremely "feminine" girl. She loved pink, was highly interested in doll play, fashion, make-up, "American Girl" paraphernalia, and creative activities related to these things. But, like most people, what she incorporated into her gender identity was flexible to a degree—she also liked Spider-Man, played football strenuously with her older brothers, and sometimes liked to accompany her brothers to play violent martial arts video games. However, she was becoming more sensitive to the unwritten rules that dictate appropriate male and female behaviors. Lia was learning our culture's **gender roles**—beliefs about what constitute appropriate behaviors for males and females. Gender roles include beliefs about what activities males and females should engage in, what jobs they ought to perform, clothing they ought to wear, and so forth.

Gender roles are not identical across the planet. For example, in some cultures, gathering wood and plowing fields are considered masculine roles, and in other cultures, feminine roles. In most Western nations it would be scandalous for a man to wear a skirt to work—but not in traditional Scotland nor present-day India or Southeast Asia, where men frequently wear skirt-like garments. Gender roles may also differ across time, particularly in industrialized nations. As a child in the 1950s, if I went to a pediatrician, he was virtually guaranteed to be male. Now, when I take my daughters to the pediatrician, she is almost always female. Until the twentieth century, the college student role was virtually exclusively a male role in the United States, but today more U.S. women than men are entering college and receiving degrees (Freeman, 2005).

Nonetheless, in most respects there is a remarkable similarity in gender roles across cultures and historical eras (Best, 2004). As one example, warfare has been engaged in primarily by men throughout history in all cultures, while care of infants and young children has been primarily expected of women.

Transgender ▶ An umbrella term of identity referring to any and all situations where a person is unhappy in the gender to which he or she was assigned at birth.

Gender roles ▶ Social beliefs about what constitute appropriate behaviors for males and females—what activities they should engage in, jobs they should perform, clothing they should wear, and so forth.

▲ **There Are Exceptions to Every Generalization about Gender Roles.** Throughout the world, combat is engaged in primarily (but not exclusively) by men, and infants and small children are cared for primarily (but not exclusively) by women. Pictured here are an Israeli platoon commander (left) and an American father (right)—two exceptions to the generalization.

Gender Stereotypes Are Beliefs about What Men and Women Are Like

Roles are a general list of appropriate behaviors for an individual in a certain category, in this case the categories "man" and "woman." A *stereotype* is more specific and narrow. It is a picture of the "typical" individual in some category. Thus, a **gender stereotype** is a belief about what a typical man or woman is like—what men and women ordinarily do, like to do, are capable of doing, and so on.

As a general rule, stereotypes allow for the efficient mental sorting and storing of information. Stereotyping is an intrinsic property of the human mind without which we might have difficulty functioning properly or even surviving. Navigating the enormous complexity of life depends upon lumping things together that share common characteristics "so that we are not flabbergasted by every new thing we encounter" (Pinker, 2002, p. 203). To some degree we *must* assume that certain things are true about objects and individuals based upon the category to which they belong (Fiske & Neuberg, 1990; Macrae, Milne, & Bodenhausen, 1994). If you are at war, and you see a person wearing a uniform of the opposing army, stereotyping relieves you of the need to ask him if he intends to shoot at you.

Nonetheless, numerous problems can arise when stereotypes are applied to human beings. Remember the "classics professor" who turned out to be a truck driver, as discussed in Chapter 9 (pp. 425–426)? The problem is that stereotypes do not really describe *people*. They are assemblies of characteristics and behaviors that often do fit a category fairly well. But within any category there are many individuals who fit the stereotype imperfectly or do not fit it at all; and some stereotypes arise not because they are a good fit to the category, but because they reflect unfounded negative social attitudes or misinformation. For example, Adolph Hitler intentionally advanced false stereotypes about Jews, gypsies, Catholics, and gay men and lesbians to rationalize the Nazi program. The same was true of 18th- and 19th-century U.S. slave owners, who advanced unfounded stereotypes of African peoples to help rationalize slave ownership.

In terms of gendered traits and behaviors, although one does usually find role-appropriate, stereotypic behavior among men and women, most members of both sexes possess at least some proportion of characteristics frequently associated with the other sex. Most people are not purely "masculine" or "feminine" in behavior, but have a mixture of these qualities. Flexibility is

Gender stereotypes ▶ Social beliefs about how a "typical" man or woman behaves. Gender stereotypes could include a person's interests, capabilities, appearance, tendencies, and so forth.

one of the qualities that have made human beings relatively successful as a species, and it enriches one's life to be able to access masculine and feminine aspects of one's character.

IN SUMMARY

1. There are four determinants of sex at birth—chromosomal, gonadal, genital, and hormonal.

2. The term *intersex* refers to a number of unusual conditions where (a) a genetic male (XY) infant is born with the appearance of female genitals, or a genetic female (XX) infant is born with the appearance of male genitals; or (b) an infant is born with aspects of both male and female gonads and genital tissue.

3. The term *gender* is usually used to refer to any aspect of male or female that is considered to be primarily social or psychological, and not biological in nature. However, maleness and femaleness contain biological, social, and psychological aspects, and many researchers have come to believe that it is not productive to use separate terms to describe sex and gender.

4. Gender identity generally does not develop until well into the third year of life. Both gender schema theory and evolutionary theory contribute to an understanding of how and why gender identity develops.

5. A transsexual is a person who identifies with the sex other than the one to which he or she was assigned at birth, and ultimately takes at least some steps to present himself or herself as a person of the other sex. Transgender is an umbrella term that can refer to any and all situations where a person's gender identity differs in some way from normative expectations based upon the sex that the person was assigned at birth.

6. Gender roles are beliefs about how men and women ought to behave—for example, what activities they should engage in and what jobs they should perform. Gender stereotypes are beliefs about how the "typical" man or woman actually behaves.

RETRIEVE!

1. Why did the term *gender* come to be used in place of *sex* in many contexts? Name one potential benefit and one potential problem resulting from the practice of creating two categories, sex and gender.

2. Why is female the "default sex" for human beings—the sex each embryo is poised to become in a genetic (chromosomal) sense?

3. True or false: A transsexual is any individual who is unhappy with the gender to which he or she was assigned at birth.

4. A child's mental "summary" of all the information he or she has acquired about gender is known as the _____.

a) gender template   c) gender prototype

b) gender schema   d) gender stereotype

5. Name one gender role you have accepted in your daily life and one gender stereotype you hold about people in general. Name one gender role you believe you have rejected (if any) and one gender stereotype (if any) that you do not hold, but you suspect some others might.

How Do the Sexes Differ?

Virtually all theories of human behavior emphasize that men and women are similar in most ways (Hyde, 2005). Even evolutionary psychologists, who predict sex differences in certain aspects of behavior, stress that in most respects men and women should be expected to be very similar in behavior (e.g., Davies & Shackelford, 2006). Yet, as we have already seen throughout this book, men and women also differ in certain respects. We have already discussed sex differences in the brain (Chapter 2), sexual behavior (Chapter 3), aggression and affiliation (Chapter 10), and strategies for dealing with threat and stress (Chapter 11). Most of these differences are acknowledged by the majority of researchers, although strong—sometimes fiery—controversy continues to exist regarding the causes, strength, universality, and consequences of these differences.

We will now consider the least, and then the most, controversial areas of psychology about which claims of sex differences have been made: *Childhood play styles and toy preferences* (least controversial) and *cognitive performance* (most controversial).

There Are Sex Differences in Play Styles and Toy Preferences

Given that a child extracts information about gender roles and gender stereotypes from the environment, you might expect that very young children would be the most "liberal" in their beliefs and attitudes about sex and gender, while teenagers and adults would be more rigid in their ideas about gender roles. Why? Because teens and adults have had so much more exposure to social expectations about men and women over a much longer period of time, and therefore, more time to learn appropriate roles and common stereotypes.

As it turns out, the opposite is true: Very young children are the worst "gender bigots," as most egalitarian parents or childcare workers find out when they attempt to interest a group of preschool boys in doll and house play or girls in battle games (Martin & Ruble, 2009; Sinno & Killen, 2009; e.g., Banerjee & Lintern, 2000; Weisner & Wilson-Mitchell, 1990). Children become somewhat *less* rigid in their ideas and behavior about gender as they pass the age of 5, and substantially more flexible as they move into adolescence and adulthood (Ruble et al., 2009).

Consider the following vivid anecdotal example from feminist writer and mother Sara Bonnett Stein (1983):

> [My friends] the Jacobsons tried very hard to bring out [their son] Kenneth's gentleness. When Kenneth's mother gave him his first baby doll, he pulled it out of the box by one arm and then crammed it into a dump truck for a wild ride along the kitchen floor. No matter how she tried to interest Kenneth in cradling the doll or dressing it, Kenneth's fascination with dolls was confined to disjointing their limbs, cutting their hair, and opening their bodies to find their hidden mechanisms. (p. 2)

Sex-typed play and toy preferences ▶ Preferences for toys and play styles associated with either boys or girls. Sex-typed play and toy preferences emerge at early ages.

Studies have shown that infants as young as 9 to 14 months (particularly males) already show **sex-typed play and toy preferences**, and infants as young as 3 to 8 months will prefer to gaze at toys typically associated with their sex (e.g., dolls/trucks; Alexander, Wilcox, & Woods, 2009; A. Campbell, et al., 2000; Jadva, Hines, & Golombok, 2010). Childhood sex-typed play styles for boys include higher levels of "propulsive" behavior (rapid running, throwing,

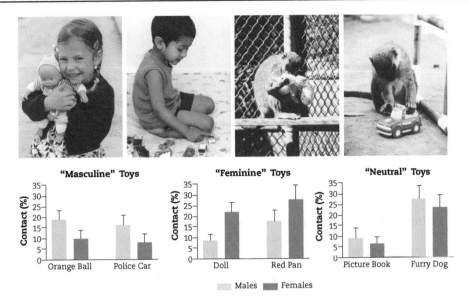

FIGURE 16.1 Sex Differences in Monkey's Play Preferences Are Similar to Those Found in Human Children. In Alexander and Hines's 2002 study, male vervet monkeys spent more time than females with "masculine" toys, but did not actually spend more time with masculine than "feminine" toys—in other words, they spent more time than females with *both* types of toys. On the other hand, female vervets did spend more time with feminine than masculine toys. *(Source: Alexander & Hines, 2002.)*

etc.), rough-and-tumble play, and preferences for toys that are easily adapted for these sorts of activities—including construction toys and "transportation" toys such as trucks. Girls' play is generally characterized by decreased physical assertion and aggression, heightened interest in play parenting (termed *alloparenting*), and play focused on interrelationships among play*mates* rather than play *objects*. Girls prefer toys that that are easily adapted to these sorts of activities (although girls' play and toy preferences are much less rigid than boys'). Finally, both girls and boys prefer to play with others of their own sex (Benenson, Liroff, Pascal, & Cioppa, 1997; Berenbaum & Hines, 1992; Knickmeyer et al., 2005; Pasterski, Geffner, Brain, Hindmarsh, & Brook, 2005; Pellegrini & Smith, 1998).

Findings that toy and play preferences begin early in infancy are particularly remarkable, because infants have not yet acquired gender identity and do not know whether they are boys or girls. In some cases, infants and toddlers come to prefer sex-typed toys before they even know how the toys are intended to be used and before they are physically developed to the point where they could possibly use the toys (Alexander et al., 2009; Jadva et al., 2010).

More surprising still are findings that sex differences seem to exist to some degree in preferences for *human* sex-typed toys among juvenile vervet and rhesus *monkeys* (Alexander & Hines, 2002; Hassett, Siebert, & Wallen, 2008)! Researchers Gerianne Alexander and Melissa Hines provided vervet monkeys with toy trucks, balls, pots, and dolls. As depicted in the graph in Figure 16.1, the male vervets spent significantly more time than the females playing with trucks and balls, while the females spent more time than the males playing with the pots and dolls.

However, in Alexander and Hines' study the toys were introduced individually to the monkeys and the amount of time the vervets spent with each toy was recorded and compared. At no time were the monkeys actually allowed to *choose* which toy they preferred. They were only allowed to play with one toy at a time. So to say that "female vervets preferred dolls over trucks," while true in one sense (time spent in play), is not true in another (choosing one toy *over* another).

This and several other problems with the Alexander and Hines study caused some people to dismiss it out of hand. However, in research designed to allow more conclusive results, Kim Wallen and several of his students allowed a group of rhesus monkeys to *choose* between wheeled toys (e.g., trucks) and plush doll-like toys (Hassett, et al., 2008). In previous research with these toys among humans, it was shown that boys vastly preferred the wheeled toys,

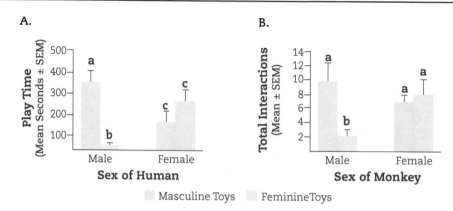

▲ **FIGURE 16.2** Graph A depicts sex differences in human children's preferences either for a wheeled toy or a plush toy, based upon research by Berenbaum and Hines (1992). In Berenbaum and Hines's study, children were given their choice of toys, and the time (in mean number of seconds) the children spent with each toy was recorded. In research designed to replicate these results using rhesus monkeys instead of children, Kim Wallen and his students found a nearly identical pattern of results, as depicted in Graph B. *(Source: Hassett et al., 2008.)*

▲ **Toys Provide "Affordances."** Children may prefer sex-typed toys because they know from past use that the toys provide certain kinds of experiences, or because the toys look as though they *might* provide these kinds of experiences (A. Campbell et al., 2000.).

Affordances ▶ A quality of any object (such as a toy) that allows for specific types of experiences.

while girls (to a somewhat lesser extent) preferred the plush toys (Berenbaum & Hines, 1992). As depicted in Figure 16.2, this pattern of human sex differences was virtually duplicated by the rhesus monkeys in the study by Wallen and his students: Male rhesus monkeys greatly preferred the wheeled toys, while females somewhat preferred the plush toys.

What's going on here? Obviously, juvenile monkeys have even less of a sense of gender identity than human infants, and they cannot possibly understand the symbolic meanings or uses of the toys they preferred. So why did they prefer them? Sex and gender researcher Anne Campbell and her colleagues (A. Campbell et al., 2000) provide a possible explanation for human children's toy preferences that can be applied to sex differences in nonhuman primates' play preferences. It may be that toys favored by boys and toys favored by girls provide intrinsically different kinds of rewarding experiences, or **affordances**. For example, the average boy appears to prefer "propulsive" activity more than the average girl; therefore, boys may be attracted to toys that they know from experience afford this kind of activity, or toys that merely look as though they *might* afford such activity, such as sticks, balls, and devices that move through space, like trucks.

Some of the sex differences in general behavior found among juvenile vervet and rhesus monkeys are similar to those found in humans (e.g., females spend more time with infants, males engage in more rough-and-tumble activity; Hassett et al., 2008). Therefore, at least some human toys may afford the monkeys experiences that are similar to those the toys afford human children. In other words, it is not the *toys* that are preferred by the monkeys—or the children—it is the type of *experiences* the toys are likely to provide.

HOMES AND HORMONES: EXPLAINING SEX DIFFERENCES IN PLAY AND TOY PREFERENCES

Even if the speculative ideas about human and nonhuman primate play preferences just discussed turn out to be correct, the question would still remain: *Why* do boys on average prefer propulsive and rough and tumble play, while girls prefer less active play and play parenting? It is generally agreed that this question has no simple answer, and none of the theories yet advanced is likely to resolve this question fully (Pasterski et al., 2005).

However, two general approaches have provided important research. The first approach stresses the importance of the infant's early *social interactions* and home life. The second stresses the effects of prenatal exposure to hormones.

Homes Recall from Chapter 3 that children may model the behaviors of important adults or older children whom they admire. Young boys may be more likely to choose older boys and men as models, and girls more likely to choose older girls and women. If older children and adults display sex-typed behavior (for whatever reasons), these behaviors may be modeled by the child and expressed as play and toy preferences (Bussey & Bandura, 1999).

The probability of this sort of modeling occurring is strengthened if the child observes the model being reinforced (rewarded) for engaging in sex-typed activity, or if the child himself or herself is reinforced. Research has demonstrated the importance of reinforcement in children's development of sex-typed play preferences. In a meta-analysis of research on parents' socialization of their boy and girl children, Hugh Lytton and David Romney (1991) found, contrary to many people's beliefs, that mothers and fathers generally do *not* socialize their sons differently from their daughters in most areas—including encouragement for achievement in various pursuits (e.g., mathematics), warmth and praise, physical and nonphysical punishment, restrictiveness or encouragement of independence, and so forth. There was a single exception, however—parents clearly *do* treat their sons differently from their daughters when it comes to play style and toys. Both girls and boys are actively encouraged to choose sex-typed toys and engage in sex-typed activities, and discouraged from deviating from sex-typed play patterns (see also Pasterski et al., 2005).

Hormones Another approach is taken by researchers such as Kim Wallen, Melissa Hines, Rebecca Knickmeyer, and several others who specialize in examining the effects of steroid hormones on behavior (e.g.,Herman & Wallen, 2007; Hines, 2004, 2006). According to researchers such as Wallen and Hines, an infant's level of prenatal (prior to birth) exposure to androgens and estrogens organizes the fetal brain in ways that are expressed in infancy and childhood as play preferences. Most research has focused on the "masculinizing" effects of prenatal exposure to androgens, particularly *testosterone* (Auyeung et al., 2009; Hines, 2006; Meyer-Bahlburg et al., 2004).

Researchers usually study this question in one of two ways. The first method is to intentionally alter levels of prenatal androgens in samples of rodents or nonhuman primates. Investigators using this approach have shown repeatedly that exposing female mammals to testosterone prenatally causes these females to engage in play and mating behavior typical of males of their species. Similarly, preventing males from being exposed to ordinary levels of androgens causes these offspring to engage in play and mating behavior typical of females (Collaer & Hines, 1995; Hines, 2006; Hotchkiss, Ostby, Vandenbergh, & Gray, 2003; Wallen, 1996).

Obviously, it would be unethical to alter the hormonal environment of human embryos and fetuses. Researchers wishing to investigate the effects of prenatal hormones on human children's play have generally adopted a different strategy: They have studied boys and girls who had unusual prenatal hormonal experiences or who were born with congenital hormonal disorders such as **congenital adrenal hyperplasia (CAH)**. CAH may result in (among other things) an overproduction of androgens such as testosterone. In particular, girls with CAH have been of interest to researchers because they have been prenatally exposed to unusually high levels of androgens and, as a result, are born with genitals that are to some degree "masculinized" (Pasterski et al., 2005; Wudy, Dorr, Solleder, Djalali, & Homoki, 1999).

Relative to normally developed girls, CAH girls also have been found to have increased preference for male sex-typed toys, games, and hobbies. They are more physically aggressive, and less interested in dolls, female playmates, infant care, or the prospect of becoming mothers themselves. As children

▲ **Like Father, Like Son.** Contrary to many people's beliefs, parents generally do not socialize boys and girls differently—but when it comes to sex-typed play activities, they do. In particular, parents (especially fathers) discourage boys from pursuing stereotypically feminine pursuits and reward them for masculine activities and preferences (*Sources: Lytton & Romney, 1991; Pasterski et al., 2005.*)

Congenital adrenal hyperplasia (CAH) ▶ A congenital hormonal disorder resulting in a greater (or sometimes lesser) production of sex steroids by the adrenal glands. Researchers have been particularly interested in CAH girls who have experienced unusual prenatal levels of exposure to androgens such as testosterone.

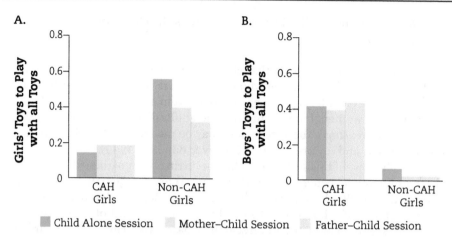

▲ **FIGURE 16.3** **Parents Encourage CAH Girls to Play with "Girl Toys," Not "Boy Toys."** As these graphs show, in the study by Pasterski and her colleagues, CAH girls were far more likely than non-CAH girls to play with "boy toys" and much less likely to play with "girl toys," whether playing alone or with a parent. Observations of play sessions also showed that both mothers and fathers provided positive feedback to both CAH and non-CAH girls for playing with sex-typed "girl" toys. However, the CAH girls received more—not less—of this feedback. Therefore, the masculinized play preferences of the CAH girls cannot be explained by parents' encouraging them to play with male sex-typed toys, because parents apparently take pains to encourage sex-typed "girl play" in CAH girls. *(Source: Graph adapted from Pasterski et al., 2005, p. 272.)*

they are more masculine in appearance and more likely to be labeled "tomboys." Moreover, the greater a girl's prenatal exposure to androgens, the more these sorts of characteristics are seen as she develops (Collaer & Hines, 1995; Meyer-Bahlburg et al., 2004; Nördenstrom, Servin, Bohlin, Larsson, & Wedell, 2002; Pasterski et al., 2005).

More powerful evidence of the importance of prenatal hormonal exposure comes from a study by Bonnie Auyeung and her research team, which included Melissa Hines and Rebecca Knickmeyer. These researchers first directly measured the amount of circulating testosterone in the amniotic fluid of 212 pregnant mothers. The fetus is perpetually bathed in amniotic fluid, and fetal testosterone is secreted into the fluid when the fetus urinates. Over a 4-year period beginning after the children reached age 6, Auyeung and her colleagues collected measures of sex-typed behavior in the children. They found that levels of prenatal testosterone directly predicted the extent of "boy-like" play behavior in the children (Auyeung et al., 2009).

One particular effect of the social environment that sometimes has been cited to explain the masculinized behavior of CAH girls is the possibility that parents might actually treat CAH girls differently because of their children's masculine appearance and their expectations for masculine behavior from their children. In other words, these parents might treat their CAH girls *like* boys because they resemble boys.

In a unique study, Vickie Pasterski and her colleagues (Pasterski et al., 2005) furnished a room with sex-typed toys and neutral toys. They allowed groups of girls and boys with and without CAH to play in the rooms either alone, with their mothers, or with their fathers. They also closely observed the play sessions to note whether the children were encouraged or discouraged from sex-typed play. As depicted in the graph in Figure 16.3, Pasterski and her colleagues found that the CAH girls were very strongly encouraged to play with the "girl toys"—even more so than were the non-CAH girls. Rather than reinforcing the masculinized preferences of the CAH girls, both mothers and fathers were attempting to *counteract* these preferences. Yet the CAH girls remained resolute in their interest in the male-typical toys.

So which is the more important influence on the development of sex-typed play and toy preferences—homes or hormones? Evidence supports both ideas in different ways (Hines, 2008). It is highly likely that play and toy preferences begin to develop in each infant as a consequence of genetic and prenatal hormonal factors, but then evolve throughout infancy and childhood as these biological factors interact with the child's personal experiences and culture. As Wallen (1996) expressed it, "nature needs nurture."

Sex Differences in Cognition Favor Men and Women in Different Ways

Why do male jazz musicians release albums at a ratio of 20:1 compared with female musicians? Why are 99% of the 894 ranked chess grand masters in the world male—and why has not a single women ever become chess champion of her country? (See Chabris & Glickman, 2006; Miller, 1999.) And why do four to seven times as many men as women (or boys/girls) score in the very highest percentiles on standardized math performance tests such as the SAT and ACT, with the ratio of males to females among "perfect" scorerers being particularly lopsided in favor of males? (See Tables 16.1 and 16.2; Valla & Ceci, 2011; Wai, Cacchio, Putallaz, & Makel, 2010.)

On the other hand, why are girls' and women's average scores on tests of verbal knowledge, fluency in speaking, reading, and (especially) writing so far above the average scores of boys and men that researchers have concluded that men are at "a rather profound disadvantage" in the performance of these "basic skills" (Hedges & Nowell, 1995, p. 45; see also Ceci, Williams, & Barnett, 2009; Halpern et al., 2007; see Figure 16.4, Tables 16.1 and 16.2)? Why are girls' school and test grades in math and science courses higher on average than boys', and why do substantially more women than men enroll in—and graduate from—undergraduate college and graduate masters' degree programs? (see Figures 12.5 and 12.6; Freeman, 2005; Hyde, 2007; Lindberg, Hyde, Linn, & Petersen, 2010). Finally, why do men, in addition to outnumbering women at the very highest levels of math performance, also outnumber women at the very *lowest* levels of scoring (Ceci, et al, 2009; Valla & Ceci, 2011)?

Anyone wishing to ask questions such as those just raised needs to be forewarned: A person can dive into the research in **sex differences in cognition** and never come out alive! Answers to these questions are maddeningly complex, often seemingly contradictory, and always controversial. Emotions flare.

Sex differences in cognition
▶ A field of research focused primarily upon possible sex differences in verbal, visual-spatial, and quantitative (mathematics) ability, motivation, and/or performance.

Table 16.2 Two Decades of Male-to-Female Ratios for SAT and ACT Math Scoring in the Top 0.01% Range (1 in 10,000)

The figures list the number of male scorers in the given range for each female scorer in that range. For example, a ratio of 1.00 would mean that for every male scorer in a given range there was one female.

	SAT			ACT	
	≥700 (top .01%)	800 ("Perfect" Score)		≥28 (top .01%)	≥32[1]
1991–1995	3.87	No data available	1990–1995	3.25	No data available
1996–2000	4.13	4.00	1996–2000	8.63	2.75
2001–2005	3.55	5.60	2001–2005	4.29	9.00
2006–2010	3.83	6.58	2006–2010	3.99	14.00

[1]There were insufficient data to compute a ratio for "perfect" scores (≥36) on the ACT math. (*Source: Wai et al., 2010, p. 415.*)

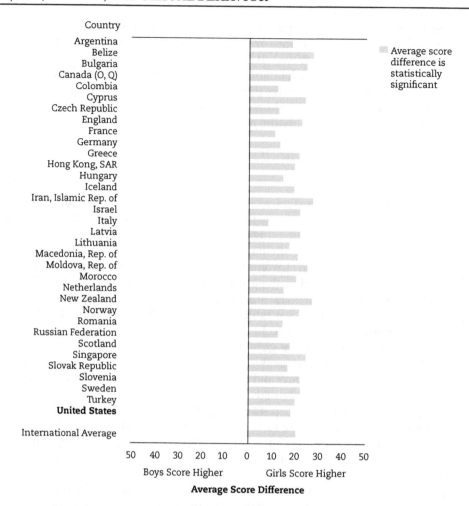

▲ **FIGURE 16.4 Throughout the World, Girls Surpass Boys in Literacy.** As shown in this chart of world sex differences in average scores for reading literacy, girls score significantly higher than boys in all 33 countries studied. Although this chart refers specifically to fourth-grade scores, results are comparable for studies of boys and girls in adolescence throughout the world. *(Source for chart: Halpern et al., 2007, p. 7. Original data from Mullis, Martin, Gonzalez, & Kennedy, 2003, and Ogle et al., 2003, cited in Halpern et al., 2007.)*

Table 16.3 Male-to-Female Ratios in SAT Writing Section Scores: 2006–2010[1]

The figures list the number of male scorers in the given range for each female scorer in that range. For example, a ratio of 0.47 would mean that there were slightly more than twice as many females for each male scorer in a given range—i.e., less than one male for each female at that range.

	≥400	≥500	≥600	≥700
2006	0.84	0.75	0.73	0.57
2007	0.81	0.71	0.69	0.61
2008	0.78	0.68	0.64	0.42
2009	0.81	0.72	0.57	0.47
2010	0.84	0.68	0.68	0.76

[1] The College Board, which created the SAT, only instituted a writing section in 2006, so no prior scores exist. *(Source: Wai et al., 2010, p. 416.)*

Field of study	1969–70	1974–75	1979–80	1984–85	1989–90	1994–95	1999–2000	2000–01
Total[1]	43.1	45.3	49.0	50.7	53.2	54.6	57.2	57.3
Agriculture and natural resources	4.1	14.1	29.6	31.1	31.6	36.0	42.9	45.1
Accounting	8.7	17.7	36.1	49.1	53.3	56.2	60.4	60.5
Biological sciences/life sciences	29.7	33.1	42.1	47.8	50.8	52.3	58.3	59.5
Business management and administrative services	9.0	16.2	33.1	44.9	46.5	47.7	49.5	49.4
Computer and information sciences	12.9	18.9	30.2	36.8	29.9	28.4	28.1	27.7
Education	75.3	73.3	73.8	75.9	78.1	75.8	75.8	76.7
Engineering	0.7	2.2	9.3	13.1	13.8	15.6	20.4	19.9
Health professions and related sciences	68.6	77.7	82.2	84.9	84.4	81.9	83.8	83.8
Mathematics	37.4	41.2	41.5	46.2	45.7	46.8	47.1	47.7
Physical sciences and science technologies	13.6	18.2	23.7	28.0	31.3	34.8	40.3	41.2
Psychology	43.4	52.6	63.3	68.2	71.5	72.9	76.5	77.5
Social sciences and history	35.9	37.3	43.6	44.1	44.2	46.8	51.2	51.8

Percent of bachelor's degrees conferred to females, by selected fields of study: Various years, 1969–70 to 2000–01

[1]Includes other fields of study not shown separately.

SOURCE: U.S. Department of Education, National Center for Education Statistics, Higher Education Genearl Information Survey (HEGIS), "Degrees and other Formal Awards Conferred Survey"; and Integrated Postsecondary Education Data System, "Completions Survey" (IPEDS-C:90-01), various years, 1989–90 through 2000–01.

▲ FIGURE 16.5 Percent of Bachelor's Degrees Earned by Women, 1969–2001. (Source: Freeman, 2005, Table 29.)

Sometimes, as happens more often than I would like as a textbook author, the same research will be cited to prove opposite points!

As an example: Take a look again at Table 16.2. Although the sex difference at the very highest levels of SAT math scoring has remained relatively constant for the past 20 years, if the time frame of the table were extended to show the past *30* years, you would have seen a dramatic drop from 1981–1985 in the ratio of male-to-female SAT math scorers in the top .05% bracket, from 13.50 to 7.60, and a further drop during the following 5 years to 3.87! This suggests that the sex gap is on its way to being eradicated, and some use this statistic to make just such a prediction.

However, researchers making this claim ignore the fact that the statistic has not budged since 1990; in fact, the male-female ratio of perfect scores on both the SAT and ACT has *increased*. (No data for perfect scores are available prior to 1990.) In the case of the ACT, the increase in the male-female ratio of perfect scoring continued from 1990–2005 just as dramatically as the top .05% ratio *decreased* on the SAT from 1980–1990! But look again—the perfect score ratio on the ACT *decreased* from 2005–2010!

Sex Differences in Cognition Might Exist in Three Ways

Sex differences in cognition can conceivably exist in any or all of three ways:

- *Ability*, a person's innate aptitude for a learning a cognitive task and performing it well in a supportive environment.
- *Motivation*, a person's interest in learning and/or performing a task.
- *Performance*, a person's scores on various tasks and tests that may—or may not—reflect innate ability and/or motivation.

Percent of master's, first-professional, and doctoral degrees conferred to females, by selected fields of study: Various years, 1969–70 to 2000–01

Degree and selected field of study	1969–70	1974–75	1979–80	1984–85	1989–90	1994–95	1999–2000	2000–01
Master's degrees	39.7	44.8	49.4	49.9	52.6	55.1	58.0	58.5
Biological sciences/life sciences	31.5	30.0	37.1	47.7	50.8	51.8	55.3	57.6
Business management	3.6	8.5	22.4	31.0	34.0	37.0	39.8	40.6
Computer and information sciences	9.3	14.7	20.9	28.7	28.1	26.1	33.3	33.9
Education	55.4	62.3	70.2	72.5	75.9	76.5	76.4	76.6
Engineering	1.1	2.4	7.0	10.7	13.8	16.3	20.7	21.2
Health professions and related sciences	52.0	61.7	72.3	76.3	77.7	78.4	77.3	77.4
Physical sciences and science techologies	14.2	14.4	18.6	23.2	26.4	30.2	35.4	36.5
Psychology	42.3	46.4	58.8	65.1	68.5	72.0	75.4	76.2
Social sciences and history	28.3	30.1	36.0	38.4	40.7	44.7	50.1	50.6
First-professional degrees[1]	5.3	12.4	24.8	32.8	38.1	40.8	44.6	45.6
Dentistry	0.9	3.1	13.3	20.7	30.9	36.4	40.1	38.6
Medicine	8.4	13.1	23.4	30.4	34.2	38.8	42.7	43.3
Law	5.4	15.1	30.2	38.5	42.2	42.6	45.9	47.3
Doctoral degrees	13.3	21.3	29.7	34.1	36.4	39.4	44.1	44.9
Business management	1.6	4.2	14.7	17.2	25.2	27.3	31.9	33.5
Biological sciences/life sciences	14.3	22.0	26.0	32.8	37.7	40.3	44.1	44.1
Computer and information sciences	1.9	6.6	11.3	10.1	14.8	18.2	16.9	17.7
Education	19.8	30.4	43.9	52.0	57.3	62.0	64.6	64.9
Engineering	0.7	2.1	3.8	6.4	8.9	11.9	15.5	16.5
Health professions and related sciences	16.2	28.6	44.7	52.9	54.2	58.1	61.2	60.9
Physical sciences and science techologies	5.4	8.3	12.4	16.2	19.4	23.5	25.5	26.8
Psychology	23.3	32.1	43.4	49.6	58.9	62.6	67.4	68.3
Social sciences and history	12.8	20.8	27.0	32.2	32.9	37.7	41.2	41.4

[1]First-professional degrees are degrees awarded in the fields of dentistry (D.D.S. or D.M.D.), medicine (M.D.), optometry (O.D.), osteopathic medicine (D.O.), pharmacy (D. Phar.), podiatric medicine (D.P. M), veterinary medicine (D.V.M.), chiropactic medicine (D.C. or D.C.M.), law (J.D.), and the theological professions (M.Div. or M.H.L.).

SOURCE: U.S. Department of Education, National Center for Education Statistics, Higher Education General Information Survey (HEGIS), "Degrees and other Formal Awards Conferred Survey": and Integrated Postsecondary Education Data System, "Completions Survey" (IPEDS-C:90-01), various years, 1989–90 through 2000–01.

▲ FIGURE 16.6 Percent of Masters', Doctoral, and First-Professional Degrees Earned by Women, 1969–2001. (Source: Freeman, 2005, Table 31.)

As stated, answers to questions about sex differences in cognition can be elusive, and often require very careful research and *counterintuitive* thinking to grasp. For example, let's take the question of women in chess. The ratio of elite male to female players is astonishing, as reported earlier: 99% of grandmasters are male, and no female has ever won a world championship or championship of her country. This record is so extreme that it is unlikely to have been caused by cultural factors, such as discrimination against women in chess. Moreover, rankings in chess are essentially objective, being based entirely on the number of games a person has won. There is no "old boy network" in chess that could subtly bias rankings against women, as conceivably could be the case in employment situations such as mathematics or engineering departments at universities or in private industry (Chabris & Glickman, 2006).

However, while it might seem logical to assume from all of this that men must have a cognitive advantage in whatever skills are required for truly excelling at chess, this assumption appears to be mistaken. In a careful analysis of the largest data set pertaining to chess performances ever examined—including the performances of more than 250,000 players over a 13-year period—Christopher Chabris and Mark Glickman (2006) have demonstrated that the lopsided ratio of male to female elite players in chess could exist for reasons that have nothing to do with innate sex differences in ability. Indeed, according to Chabris and Glickman's analysis, the reason there are so many more highly accomplished male than female chess players is that far many more boys than girls enter chess competition at the lowest levels at early ages. Because so many more boys than girls enter competitive chess early on, the poorer male players are soon weeded out. By the time higher level competitive games are played, a very small pool of accomplished female players competes against an enormous pool of only the very best male players.

Of course, this analysis still leaves unanswered the question of why so many more boys than girls learn and play chess in the first place. There does appear to be a sex difference in *motivation* to play chess. But what is the origin of the difference in motivation? Is it that chess is perceived to be a "boy thing," so that most girls and their parents are reluctant to become involved? Or, as in play and toy preferences, is this sex difference in motivation possibly innate and determined by the type of experience chess affords? *Ability, performance*, and *motivation*—these factors are often intertwined in ways that make it difficult to disentangle them (Ceci et al., 2009; Halpern et al., 2007).

QUANTITATIVE, VISUAL-SPATIAL, AND VERBAL PERFORMANCE

In any event, regardless of how much of the sex differences in performance on cognitive tasks and tests is due to differences in innate ability, motivation, or social factors (as discussed in *Critical Thinking about Psychology*, for example), it is still the case that these differences are well established (Geary, 2010; Halpern et al., 2007; Valla & Ceci, 2011). Average sex differences in cognitive performance often begin in very early childhood (or even infancy), and they have remained consistent over time—that is, they do not appear to be narrowing (Ceci et al., 2009; Valla & Ceci, 2011; Wai et al., 2010; but see Lindberg, Hyde, Linn, & Petersen, 2010, for a different view).

The report by Diane Halpern and her colleagues on cognitive sex differences in science and math-related performance is a particularly important summary of this evidence, because it was authored by scientists from a wide variety of disciplines and perspectives—feminist social psychology, evolutionary psychology, developmental psychology, neuroscience, and research methods/statistics (Halpern et al., 2007). Scientists from these disciplines often disagree very strongly about the strength, causes, and implications of cognitive sex differences. That this diverse group stood united behind their conclusions suggests that the evidence supporting these conclusions is particularly strong (Barnett, 2007).

What does the evidence show? As summarized in Figure 16.7, most of the evidence pertains to differences in three areas of cognition: *verbal performance, visual-spatial performance*, and *quantitative (mathematics) performance*.

Verbal Performance **Verbal performance** includes all areas of language use and memory—knowledge of vocabulary, grammar, and spelling; reading comprehension, verbal reasoning; and speed of processing of language-related tasks (e.g., how rapidly a person can provide a correct synonym or definition of a word).

As already pointed out, all evidence shows that girls and women excel at (almost) all verbal tasks relative to boys and men, particularly writing. For example, the writing scores of *8th*-grade girls are roughly comparable to the writing scores of *11th*-grade boys (Bae, Choy, Geddes, Sable, & Snyder, 2000;

▲ **99% of Chess Grandmasters Are Male.** No female has ever won a world chess championship or championship of her country. Although this might seem to suggest that females lack chess ability relative to males, research shows otherwise. The lopsided ratio of high-performing females in chess is due to the fact that far more boys than girls enter chess competition at very early ages. The poorer male players are soon weeded out, and by adulthood only the very strongest male players remain (Chabris & Glickman, 2006).

Verbal performance ▶ Performance on tasks necessitating skill in all areas of language use and memory. May include knowledge of vocabulary, grammar, and spelling; reading comprehension; verbal reasoning; and speed of processing of language-related tasks.

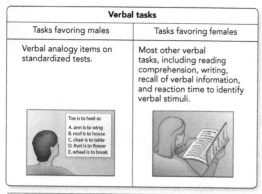

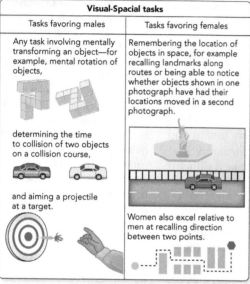

▲ **FIGURE 16.7** Average Cognitive Sex Differences in Task and Test Performance. *(Source: Adapted from Kimura, 1992, with additional data summarized by Halpern et al., 2007.)*

Visual-spatial performance

▶ Performance on tasks necessitating skills in mentally "working with" visual and spatial imagery and information.

see Table 16.3)! Moreover, as depicted in Figure 16.7, girls' literacy scores surpass those of boys throughout the world, and women are also better at memory tasks involving recall of words and objects and recollections of personal experiences described verbally (Ceci et al., 2009; Herlitz & Rehnman, 2008; Lewin, Wolgers, & Herlitz, 2001).

On the other hand, there is at least one area of verbal performance where boys score higher than girls: the sort of verbal analogy items that used to be part of the SAT and are still part of many other standardized tests (Strand, Deary, & Smith, 2006; e.g., "ennui is to enthusiasm as introversion is to . . ."). These questions are thought to tap the sort of cognitive processes used for reasoning about mathematical relationships (Halpern, 2004).

Visual-spatial Performance **Visual-spatial performance** includes the various ways that imagery is mentally constructed and "worked with" in working memory (Halpern et al., 2007). One such task would be choosing from a series of possible examples how a given three-dimensional image would look if it were rotated in space in various ways (see Figure 16.8). Another visual-spatial task involves making judgments about moving objects—for example, estimating how long it would take two objects moving toward one another to collide; or determining the correct trajectory for hitting a target from a given distance.

Males' average visual-spatial superiority emerges reliably in boys as young as 4 (Halpern, 2004), and two independent research teams were able to demonstrate superior mental rotation ability in male infants as young as 3 and 4 months (D. S. Moore & Johnson, 2008; P. C. Quinn & Liben, 2008)! It is visual-spatial ability alone that is likely responsible for males outperforming females at the very highest end of mathematics achievement scores on standardized tests, as I will describe in the next section (Casey, Nuttall, Pezaris, & Benbow, 1995).

Males do not have an advantage over women in all visual-spatial tasks, however. Women outperform men in their ability to recall the location of objects, including memory for landmarks when learning new routes, or recall of directions between two points (making men's famous reluctance to ask for directions when lost rather ironic; Ceci et al., 2009; Eals & Silverman, 1994; Galea & Kimura, 1993).

Quantitative Performance Sex differences in **quantitative performance** (mathematics tasks) have probably received the most attention from the media. But the picture is much more complex than is usually presented. For example, girls' math (and science) class grades—and their scores on tests of curriculum for these classes—are consistently *higher* than boys'. In particular, girls show an advantage in class test arithmetic scores during the elementary school years, a time when the skills necessary for solving math problems primarily involve memorization and calculation techniques—tapping cognitive processes similar to those used for language comprehension (Halpern et al., 2007; Wei et al., 2012). Girls' math advantages are also seen in later grades in

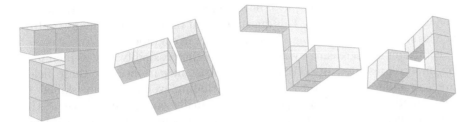

▲ **FIGURE 16.8 Mental Rotation: A Test of Visual-Spatial Ability.** The test here is to determine how the two figures labeled A and the two figures labeled B could be rotated in space to make them identical (Halpern et al., 2007, p. 9). A sex difference in mental rotation ability has been demonstrated by two independent research teams in infants as young as 3 and 4 months (D. S. Moore & Johnson, 2008; P. C. Quinn & Liben, 2008). *(Source: Halpern et al., 2007.)*

scores on standardized tests for certain types of algebra problems where the solution strategies also involve cognitive processing skills similar to those used for language (Gallagher, Levin, & Cahalan, 2002).

In all other aspects of mathematical performance beginning in later grades, however—particularly in geometry and other sorts of math problems involving visual-spatial skills—males consistently score higher in standardized tests, particularly at the very highest levels, as explained earlier. The greater representation of late-adolescent males at the very highest levels of math performance on standardized tests follows a pattern that is also seen in early childhood: More preschool boys than girls are identified as mathematically gifted (Casey et al., 1995; Hedges & Nowell, 1995; Robinson, Abbott, Berninger, & Busse, 1996).

However, it is also the case that male scores in quantitative tests are more *variable* than those of females. This means that men outnumber women at the very *lowest* end of scoring, as well as the highest. The origin of this lowest-highest variability in males' math scoring is unknown, although theories abound.

Quantitative performance
▶ Performance on tasks necessitating mathematics skills.

To Some Extent, It All Depends on the Task As you can see, although one often hears that "women are better in verbal and men are better in visual-spatial and math," this generalization is not completely true. To some extent, average sex differences in cognition depend upon the specific task. This underscores the extent to which the three areas—verbal, visual-spatial, and quantitative—are interrelated as well as being distinct. For example, it takes verbal ability to solve mathematics problems stated in verbal terms, and it takes visual-spatial ability to solve certain types of verbal problems involving memory for the placement of objects one has seen in pictures.

Interestingly, average differences between men and women, even those that have persisted over decades, may be amenable to change through training. A unique example of this was provided by researcher Jing Feng and colleagues (Feng, Spence, & Pratt, 2007). These researchers found that playing an action video game involving shooting at moving targets (*Medal of Honor: Pacific Assault*) for a total of 10 hours over a 4-week period reduced sex differences in performance on high-level visual-spatial tasks, including mental rotation tasks. As the research team points out, these skills are important for successful performance in math and science courses, on standardized tests, as a math or science major in college, and in so-called STEM fields (science, technology, engineering, or technology) in which women are famously underrepresented (Ceci et al., 2009).

On the other hand, the research team also observed that boys ordinarily receive this training via action video games, and girls do not, because boys—and not girls—are *motivated* to play these games. Here again we are faced with

the problem of determining *why* boys and girls are differently motivated to engage in various activities. This question sits at the heart of the many controversies surrounding the topic of sex differences in cognition.

For example, increasing evidence suggests the possibility that women may be underrepresented in STEM fields at least in part because these fields are less interesting to most women—including women highly skilled in mathematics—than other types of intellectually challenging careers. The relative dearth of women in these fields does not seem to have resulted from any purported discrimination in hiring, admissions to graduate programs, or grant applications (Ceci & Williams, 2010; National Research Council, 2010; Su, Rounds, & Armstrong, 2009; Valla & Ceci, 2011). Instead, the stereotype of women being more interested in working with *people* and men more interested in working with *things* appears to have at least a measure of truth (Su et al., 2009). Because women highly skilled in mathematics are more likely than their male peers also to possess high levels of verbal ability, they may be faced with a wider universe of career choices, and this may allow women greater flexibility to express their true preferences (Ceci & Williams, 2010).

CRITICAL THINKING ABOUT PSYCHOLOGY

Stereotype Threat: Are Scientific Theories about Sex Differences Dangerous?

In January of 2005, then-president of Harvard University Lawrence Summers made several comments during a speech that ultimately led to his resignation. He suggested that women were seriously underrepresented in science and engineering fields—particularly at the "higher end" of performance in these fields—and that this underrepresentation might be explained by innate sex differences in science- and math-related cognitive abilities and interests.

Anyone involved in academic life during these years knows about the fiery controversy that followed, with numerous groups and individuals calling for Summers' resignation. It was not Summers' claim that women are underrepresented in science and math fields which created the explosion of criticism. Although women currently earn over 68% of all doctoral degrees in psychology and almost as many in education, they earn only 16.5% of doctoral degrees in engineering and 26.8% in physical sciences and technology (see Figure 16.9). As Figure 16.9 shows, even when matched for high math ability, women are far less likely than their male counterparts to go into mathematics, science, or engineering careers (Benbow, Lubinski, Shea, & Eftekhari-Sanjani, 2000).

Instead, those who were angered by Summers' speech argued that there was no scientific basis for his suggestion that men and women might differ in math- and science-related *abilities*. They also argued that such notions, coming as they did from a person in academic authority, might discourage women from seeking the very careers in which they currently are in short supply. In other words, Summers' remarks were thought by some of his critics to be *dangerous*.

Researchers Ilan Dar-Nimrod and Steven J. Heine (2006) tested this idea, using a research strategy related to stereotype threat. **Stereotype threat** is a reduction in task or test performance when negative stereotypes about the sex or minority group to which a person belongs are "activated" in his or her own mind (Steele & Aronson, 1995). Once activated, the person "monitors" himself or herself for signs of failure or confirmation of the stereotype. The person becomes preoccupied with suppressing these negative thoughts, taking needed resources from where they belong—the task at hand (Schmader, 2010).

Stereotype threat ▶ Reduced task or test performance when negative stereotypes about the sex or minority group to which a person belongs are activated in his or her own mind.

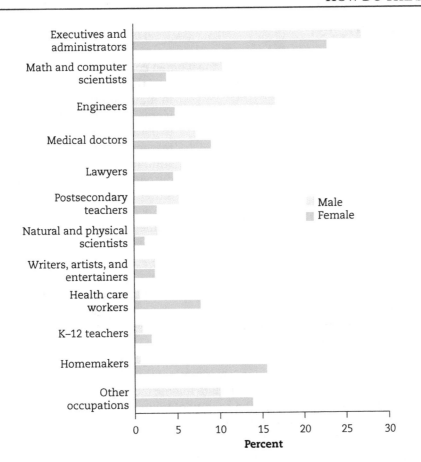

◄FIGURE 16.9 Eventual Career Choices of Mathematically Gifted Boys and Girls. Boys and girls who were equally gifted in mathematics ability, scoring in the top 1%, showed some significant differences in the careers they eventually pursued—although a large number of both males and females became executives and administrators. *(Source: Halpern et al., 2007/2008, p. 51.)*

Stereotype threat has been demonstrated in women's performances on tests. For example, women's math performance has been shown to suffer when negative stereotypes about women and math were activated while the women heard or read statements suggesting that women's scores on the test they were about to take tended to be lower than men's (D. M. Quinn & Spencer, 2001). While testing under these conditions, women may experience increasingly negative thoughts about the test, mathematics in general, and their own ability to perform well (Cadinu, Maass, Rosabianca, & Kiesner, 2005). Thus, women's decreased performance under stereotype threat tends to show up toward the later portions of math tests—after such thoughts have had an opportunity to simmer and have a pernicious effect.

Dar-Nimrod and Heine wanted to test the possibility that reading different ideas about the causes of sex differences in math performance might strengthen or lessen the effects of stereotype threat. The researchers gave four groups of women a test similar to the Graduate Record Exam (GRE), which includes math and reading comprehension sections. However, the reading comprehension section consisted of an essay which differed for each group of women. As depicted in the graph in Figure 16.10, one group read an essay which claimed that there were no sex differences at all in math ability or performance. A second group read an essay claiming that performance differences did exist, but they were entirely due to experiences in society (such as sexist expectations of teachers). A third group read an essay which claimed that differences in math ability were innate and due to genetics. The fourth group read an essay that did not refer to math ability at all, but merely "primed" the reader to think about sex/gender by discussing the history of the female body in art.

CRITICAL THINKING ABOUT PSYCHOLOGY

CONTINUED

▶ FIGURE 16.10 Reading about Theories of Sex Differences Affects Women's Math Performance. In the study by Dar-Nimrod and Heine (2006), women who read essays which claimed that no sex differences in math ability existed (labeled *no difference* or ND in the graph), or essays proclaiming that such differences did exist but were entirely the result of social experiences (labeled *experiential* or E), performed better on math tests than women who read essays suggesting that sex differences in math ability were genetic (labeled *genetics* or G). Women who read essays that did not refer to math ability at all, but primed the women to think about sex/gender (labeled *standard stereotype threat* or S), performed similarly to those who read the "genetic" explanation. These results suggest that stereotype threat can be reduced if women are presented with environmental explanations of sex differences prior to taking a math test.

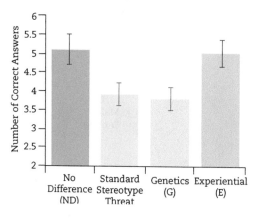

After reading their assigned essays, the women completed a math test. As you can see in Figure 16.10, women who read the "no sex differences in math ability" essay and women who read the "social experience causes sex differences" essay performed similarly on the test—and both outperformed those who read either the "genetic causes" essay or the essay that simply primed thoughts about sex/gender.

However, you will also note that women reading the "genetic" and "primed to think about sex/gender" essays also performed similarly. Why did women who were only primed to think about sex and gender score similarly to those who read the "genetics" essay? The authors reasoned that women as a rule probably tend to accept the stereotype that women have lower math ability that men, and that the explanation is probably rooted in innate female biology (genetics). Merely referring to sex and gender in the context of taking a math test is thus equal to reading an essay explicitly presenting the genetics position. This is the essence of stereotype threat.

Of course, no one suggests that women's underrepresentation at the higher levels of science, engineering, and math fields is due to stereotype threat—for example, stereotype threat primarily shows up in laboratory studies and less so (if at all) in real-life testing situations where in most instances women are not primed to think about sex or gender (Cullen, Hardison, & Sackett, 2004; Stricker & Ward, 2004). And, in any case, standardized testing scores are not the only factor bearing upon a person's life choices, career, and job performance (Halpern et al., 2007).

However, results of studies such as Dar-Nimrod and Heine's raise uncomfortable questions about the nature of scientific inquiry and the responsibilities of scientists, as Dar-Nimrod and Heine suggest. Are genetic explanations of sex differences in ability dangerous? This question is not answered easily and views tend toward the extreme. ■

IN SUMMARY

1. Males and females behave similarly in most ways, but some consistent differences exist. In general, boys prefer higher levels of "propulsive" and rough-and-tumble play, and they like toys that may be easily adapted for these activities. Girls generally prefer play characterized by decreased physical assertion and aggression. They frequently enjoy alloparenting (play parenting) and play focused upon interrelationships among playmates rather than play objects. They prefer toys that may be adapted to these uses. Both sexes prefer same-sex playmates.

2. Sex differences in play and toy preferences may emerge in part as a result of social interactions and in part as a result of prenatal exposure to androgens and estrogens.

3. Sex differences in cognitive performance exist in children and adults. Some of these differences begin to emerge in early childhood or even infancy. Differences exist in verbal, visual-spatial, and quantitative (mathematics) performance.

4. Although females in general have been found to excel in verbal tasks and males in visual-spatial and quantitative tasks, to some extent the nature of the difference—favoring females or favoring males—will depend upon the specific verbal, visual-spatial, and quantitative task. Moreover, it is not always clear how much of the observed sex differences in cognitive performance result from differences in ability or motivation, or both; or from social influences such as stereotype threat.

RETRIEVE!

1. What was the explanation provided by "affordances" theory (Anne Campbell) for why both boy and girl children and male and female monkeys might prefer sex-typed toys?

2. True or False: According to research, CAH-girls are reinforced by their parents for engaging in "boy-typical" play.

3. How might both hormonal and social factors play a part in the development of play and toy preferences?

4. How is it possible that there are 894 male chess grandmasters in the world and only 9 female (99% vs. 1%)—yet, there is no innate difference between male and female chess playing ability?

5. List as many areas of verbal performance as you can recall in which *males* excel. List as many areas of visual-spatial and quantitative performance as you can recall in which *females* excel. Then do the reverse: List female advantages in verbal and male advantages in visual-spatial and quantitative performance.

6. Which of the following is NOT one of the ways in which sex differences in cognition might exist?

a) ability   b) motivation   c) experience   d) performance

Sexual Behavior: What Is "Having Sex"?

Now that I have discussed *sex* as in *male* and *female*, I will devote the remainder of the chapter to exploring *sexual behavior*. It is interesting to note that although sex can be one of the most important motivators of human behavior—indeed, theories such as psychoanalysis and evolutionary psychology consider it *the* prime motivator of much of human behavior—less is known about the psychology of human sexual behavior than virtually any other aspect of human life. This is due primarily to resistance to the study of human sexuality among scientists and funding agencies (Abramson, 1992).

▶ **Are We Having Sex Yet?** People disagree as to what constitutes "having sex."

People Do Not Agree on What Constitutes "Having Sex"

What *is* "having sex"? In other words, what do we mean by "sexual behavior"? The answer is not as straightforward as it might seem. For example, some years ago, a male friend, then aged 45, was engaged to a woman 20 years his junior, whom he eventually married. He recalled to me the first time they had sex—or did they? There seemed to have been a difference of opinion on that score. After a wonderful night out at a Northern Italian restaurant neither of them could afford, a chilled bottle of Cascina Fonda Vendemmia Tardiva Moscato d'Asti, and a lot of gazing into each other's eyes, they fell into bed and passionately embraced. Within 20 minutes, they were naked, and engaging in **oral-genital sex**, the stimulating of a partner's genitals with the lips and tongue.

At one point, my friend's wife-to-be whispered breathlessly, "Is it okay if we don't have sex?" My friend paused—genuinely puzzled. "I thought that's what we were doing," he answered honestly. According to my friend's Baby Boomer upbringing, oral sex decidedly constituted "having sex." In fact, it was the most intimate form of sex imaginable—something one just did not do unless one really felt very close to one's partner and most likely already had been having *sexual intercourse* for a period of time. On the other hand, to his partner's generation, oral sex was *not* "having sex," and was far *less* intimate than sexual intercourse!

Some researchers have studied what people do and don't define as "having sex." Almost all people studied define penile-vaginal **sexual intercourse**—the insertion of a man's penis in a woman's vagina—as "having sex." However, in a number of studies conducted in the United States, Canada, the United Kingdom, and Australia, between 42% and 80% did *not* consider oral-genital contact as "having sex," and between 10% and 30% did *not* consider **anal intercourse**—insertion of the penis into a male or female partner's anus—as "having sex" (Byers, Henderson, & Hobson, 2009).

However, the picture may be a bit more complex than simply voting whether or not a behavior constitutes "having sex." For example, in one study, participants' determinations of whether or not "sex" had occurred were dependent not only on the nature of the behavior, but also on whether or not orgasm occurred. (Orgasm is the physiological and psychological "climax" of sexual activity [see pp. 801–802].) Participants in this study reported that oral sex and sexual intercourse were more likely to be considered "having sex" if one or both partners had an orgasm, and particularly if a man had an orgasm (Cecil,

Oral-genital sex ▶ Stimulating a partner's genitals with the lips or tongue. Stimulation of the penis in this way is known as *fellatio*. Stimulation of the vulva in this way is known as *cunnilingus*. Common slang for oral genital sex includes *blow job, going down, giving head,* and *blowing*.

Sexual intercourse ▶ The term generally reserved to describe insertion of a man's penis in a woman's vagina.

Anal intercourse ▶ Insertion of a man's penis in his partner's anus.

Fantasy

- Sex with a virgin
- Two or more partners simultaneously
- Anal intercourse
- Making love with the possibility of being discovered
- Seeing pictures/videos of yourself having sex
- Watching partner undress
- Sex with a much older partner
- Sex with a much younger partner
- Masturbating your partner
- Oral-genital sex
- Sex with a mysterious stranger
- Intercourse in unusual positions
- Naked caressing
- Touching/kissing sensuously
- Being forced to submit
- Being rescued from danger by one who will become lover
- Performing sex before an audience
- Homosexual fantasies
- Fantasies of being the other sex
- Getting married

■ Male
■ Female

0 10 20 30 40 50 60 70 80 90 100
Percentage

◀**FIGURE 16.11 Sexual Fantasy Is the Most Common Form of Sexual Behavior.** This chart reports some of the differences between the content of the sexual fantasies of 160 male and female heterosexual college students. The fantasies are arranged in order from those most often reported by men to those most often reported by women. *(Source: Chart adapted from LeVay & Valente, 2003, p. 217; based on data reported by Hsu, Kling, Kessler, Knapke et al., 1994.)*

Bogart, Wagstaff, Pinkerton, & Abramson, 2002). Other factors, such as the sex (gender) of the study participant and religious beliefs and activity, may also enter into these judgments (Byers et al., 2009). Moreover, participants in most of these studies were university students—older people and nonstudents may have different ideas.

Well, then, what *is* "having sex"? If you think you have a pretty good idea, consider that to a *shoe-fetishist*—a person who receives his most fulfilling sex in the context of observing or caressing specific sorts of shoes—"having sex" might consist primarily of rummaging through a stranger's shoe closet. Similarly, a practitioner of **sadism-masochism (S/M)**—the umbrella term for practices which might include pain, domination/submission, and/or bondage—might consider being tied up with Japanese hemp rope and lashed with a whip an excellent example of "having sex." On the other hand, a woman who has been raped, regardless of the fact that she has engaged in sexual intercourse, might not consider that she has had "sex" at all. Instead she might define her experience as violent assault—closer to a beating than a sex act (see the "Living Psychology" feature on page 804).

Or consider **sexual fantasy**, which does not necessarily involve any physical behavior or body parts at all, other than the brain. People may have sexual fantasies while eating breakfast, riding on the subway, shopping, sleeping, gardening, listening to boring lectures (or even interesting ones), and while masturbating (self-pleasuring)—in short, any time and any place. Without doubt, fantasy is the most common of all forms of human sexual behavior (Ellis & Symons, 1990).

Sadism-masochism (SM) ▶ A global term that includes sexual interest in providing or experiencing pain, domination, humiliation, and/or bondage.

Sexual fantasy ▶ Sexual activity in thought or mental images and reveries of a sexual nature.

Approximately 95% of Americans report having had sexual fantasies of one sort or another (Leitenberg & Henning, 1995; see also Traeen, Stigum, & Sørensen, 2002, for similar figures among Norwegians). When researchers asked 4,000 men and women between the ages of 14 and 25, "Have you thought about sex at all during the last 5 minutes?" 52% of the men and 39% of the women answered "Yes" (Cameron & Biber, 1973; see Figure 16.11). Contrary to popular belief, fantasy does *not* necessarily signal dissatisfaction with one's partner or with one's sex life. Quite the opposite: Those who report fantasizing more also report *increased* satisfaction with their sex lives, and also report having *more* sex than those who fantasize less (Leitenberg & Henning, 1995).

Thus, the term *sexual behavior* can only really be defined in a very broad and circular fashion as "any type of behavior involving feelings and responses which are thought by the participant(s) to be sexual in nature." Not very informative, I agree. But while sexual behavior is exceptionally diverse, it also expresses, in a particularly poignant way, the unity of the human species.

"HOOKING UP"

No discussion of how people define "having sex"—particularly young people—is complete without considering "hooking up." **Hooking up** is a slang term for a sexualized encounter between two strangers or brief acquaintances that may or may not include sexual intercourse; an earlier term with similar meaning is "one-night stand." Hookups usually occur on only one occasion (Paul, McManus, & Hayes, 2000, p. 76). Hookups should not be confused with *friends with benefits*—a nonromantic friendship in which the participants sometimes engage in sexual behavior for fun or other reasons (Hughes, Morrison, & Asada, 2005).

The frequency, seeming casualness, and relative social acceptability of teenagers' hookups are incomprehensible to many older adults, but they are engaged in at least once a year by the majority of college students in the United States (Owen, Rhoades, Stanley, & Fincham, 2010; Paul et al., 2000). Why do many older adults have such a difficult time understanding hooking up? In the early 20th century, dating relationships proceeded according to specific steps and stages (Owen et al., 2010). Women were warned "not to kiss on the first date," but for people "going steady," kissing (and more, depending on circumstances) was just fine—especially if class rings or other tokens of commitment were exchanged. Stages, steps, and symbolic gestures such as these have become extinct, and boundaries of sexual behavior in high school and college have become ambiguous.

In Chapter 3 we looked at sex differences in interest in casual sex—which, unlike hooking up, specifically refers to sexual intercourse. Are there similar sex differences in interest in, or the experience of, hookups? Women are more likely than men to regret hooking up and to have had a negative emotional reaction, particularly if the hookup included intercourse and the partner was a person the woman had known for less than 24 hours (Eshbaugh & Gute, 2008; Owen et al., 2010; Townsend & Wasserman, 2011). In a large-scale study by Jesse Owen and colleagues, almost 50% of women reported primarily negative reactions, and only 26% responded positively. This is a virtual mirror image of the results for men, 50% of whom reported *positive* responses and 26% of whom reported negative responses. (The remaining one-quarter of the male and female samples were "ambivalent.") This is consistent with most research on sex differences in casual sex overall (Okami & Shackelford, 2001; see Chapter 3).

Interestingly, research paints a general picture of false assumptions about hooking up among college students. While men correctly believe that women are less comfortable with hooking up than are men—and women correctly agree—both sexes overestimate just how comfortable the other sex actually is

---

Hooking up ▶ A sexualized encounter between two strangers or brief acquaintances that may or may not include sexual intercourse. Hookups usually occur on only one occasion.

Human sexual response ▶ The process by which a person becomes sexually aroused, experiences orgasm (or not, as the case may be), and returns to a pre-aroused state.

Human sexual response cycle ▶ Models of human sexual response. The first such model was created by William Masters and Virginia Johnson in 1966.

Vaginal lubrication ▶ Slippery, clear, and fragrant fluid secreted on the walls of the vagina during sexual excitement.

Penile erection ▶ Engorgement of the spongy columns of the penis with blood during sexual excitement.

Plateau ▶ The second stage of the sexual response cycle representing peak excitement levels. Although Masters and Johnson applied this stage both to men and women, evidence suggests that only women experience plateau—marked by the retraction of the clitoris beneath the clitoral hood and the formation of the orgasmic platform.

in hookups. In other words, both men and women are not as happy with the custom as the other sex thinks they are. Moreover, both men and women assume that other members of their own sex are more comfortable with hooking up than they are themselves (Reiber & Garcia, 2010)!

The Physiology of Sexual Response Proceeds in Stages

Until 1966, the general public knew virtually nothing about the physiology of **human sexual response**—the process by which a person becomes sexually aroused, experiences orgasm (or not, as the case may be), and returns to the pre-aroused state. In that year, a medical doctor and his secretary/collaborator (and eventual wife) published the first detailed account of the physiology of human sexual response (Masters & Johnson, 1966). Eventually, the names William Masters and Virginia Johnson, with their white coats and air of scientific authority, came to exemplify in the public mind the entire field of sex research and sex therapy. During the 1950s and 1960s, Masters and Johnson actually observed, filmed, and took physiological measurements of many hundreds of volunteers engaged in thousands of instances of common types of sexual activities. The result of all this measuring and filming was their proposed four-stage *human sexual response cycle.*

Masters and Johnson attempted to create a "one-size-fits-all" cycle that would apply equally to men and women. However, the sexual response of men and women, while similar in many respects, is not identical (Salonia et al., 2010). Therefore, various other researchers have tinkered with Masters and Johnson's model over the years to make it more realistic (see Robinson, 1989 for a detailed critique of Masters and Johnson).

Masters and Johnson's original model of the **human sexual response cycle** consisted of four stages: *excitement, plateau, orgasm,* and *resolution.*

Excitement is initial sexual arousal. In women, the most obvious physical sign of excitement is the production of a slippery, clear, and fragrant fluid on the walls of the vagina, much like sweat glands produce perspiration. This process is known as **vaginal lubrication**. In men, the most obvious physical sign of the excitement phase is **penile erection**. Erection occurs as a result of expansion of the arteries leading into the penis, and consequent engorgement of the spongy columns of the penis with blood. (That's right, there are no bones in the human penis, it's all blood and soft tissue!) In both women and men, the excitement phase is marked by an increase in heart rate, blood pressure, and bodily muscle tension.

Plateau represents the maintenance of peak excitement levels. Strictly speaking, plateau only applies to women, although Masters and Johnson included it in their model for both sexes. During this stage the clitoris decreases up to 50% in length, and retracts beneath the **clitoral hood**—a stretch of protective tissue. The outer third of the vagina forms a tube-like tightening called the **orgasmic platform**. There is further increase in heart rate, respiration, blood pressure, and muscle tension.

Orgasm is the physiological and psychological climax of the sexual response cycle. Orgasm in men is accompanied by ejaculatory contractions which expel sperm-containing semen from the penis. In women, orgasmic contractions occur in pelvic structures from the vagina to the uterus. Women's orgasm is most reliably triggered by direct or indirect stimulation of the clitoris, or by pressure against certain areas of the vaginal walls. In both women and men, heart rate during orgasm can be extraordinarily high. There is often a general loss of voluntary muscle and motor control.

Resolution is the return to a nonaroused state. In men, there is gradual return of the penis to normal size and flaccidity, and return of heart rate, respiration, and muscle tension to pre-excitement levels. At this point most men experience the onset of the **refractory period**, during which they are unable to attain an erection. This period may last from one or two minutes to several

Clitoral hood ▶ A stretch of protective tissue surrounding the clitoris.

Orgasmic platform ▶ A tube-like tightening of the outer third of the vagina during the plateau phase of the sexual response cycle.

Orgasm ▶ The psychological and physiological "climax" of sexual activity as described in the sexual response cycle. Orgasm is characterized by intense physical pleasure and euphoria, muscle contraction and spasm, and sharply increased heart rate and respiration. Orgasm in men is followed by a refractory (rest) period, but women may experience additional successive serial orgasms.

Resolution ▶ The stage of the sexual response cycle where a person returns to a nonaroused state.

Refractory period ▶ The postorgasm period for men, during which a man is unable to achieve an erection. The refractory period may last from minutes to days, depending upon the man's age, health, how often he has been engaging in sex, and the degree to which he is attracted to his partner.

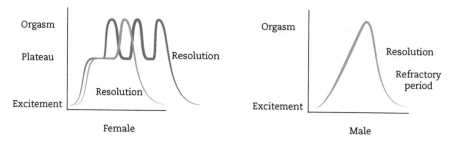

▲ **FIGURE 16.12 Sexual Response Cycles of Men and Women.** Depicted here are modified versions of Masters and Johnson's sexual response cycle. Women's cycle includes *excitement, plateau, orgasm,* and *resolution*. These stages may include *serial orgasm* (red line), in which the woman returns directly to plateau and experiences additional orgasms, each time returning to plateau—resolving only after the final orgasm. The male cycle does not include a plateau stage; instead, men's excitement levels continue to rise until orgasm. On the other hand, men go through a stage that women do not: the *refractory period*.

days, depending on the man's age, health, how often he has been engaging in sex, and the degree to which he is attracted to his partner.

In women, either of two things may happen in the resolution phase. There may be a complete return of heart rate, respiration, blood pressure, and so forth to pre-arousal levels; or there may be only a partial resolution (or virtually no resolution) and, instead, a second orgasm . . . and possibly a third, fourth, and so on—a phenomenon known as **serial orgasms**. Figure 16.12 depicts modified versions of typical sexual response cycles for men and women separately.

Finally, women's experience of sexual response does not include the orgasm phase as reliably as does men's (Wallen, 2011). Although men do not always orgasm either, they do so with amazing regularity as compared with women. For example, in the first large, representative national survey of sexuality in the United States, only 60% of women reported that they "usually or always" experienced orgasm during masturbation compared with 80% of men; and only 29% of women reported usually or always experiencing orgasm during sex with a partner compared with 75% of men (Laumann, Gagnon, Michael, & Michaels, 1994). In a later, international survey of men and women in 29 countries, between 10% and 34% of women reported a periodic or frequent inability to reach orgasm; in contrast, the figure for men was 5% to 15% (Laumann et al., 2005). Orgasm problems are also the second most common sexual complaint of women in the United States (Meston, Levin, Sipski, Hull, & Heiman, 2004). However, it is interesting to note that, contrary to what some might think, difficulties with orgasm do not necessarily result in a woman's dissatisfaction with her sexual life or relationship (Graham, 2010).

MEN'S AND WOMEN'S AROUSAL PATTERNS MAY ALSO DIFFER

In addition to the differences in men's and women's sexual response cycles just discussed, there are more general differences in how men and women become aroused. Research conducted by Meredith Chivers and her colleagues has shown that women can become aroused by sexual stimuli—such as images and videos—that are not specific to their actual sexual interests, whereas men require stimuli that are specific to their sexual interests. Moreover, women's *physiological* (genital) arousal may not necessarily be accompanied by *subjective feelings* of arousal—whereas men's genital arousal is rarely disconnected from their subjective feelings of arousal (Chivers & Bailey, 2005; Chivers, Seto, Lalumière, Laan, & Grimbos, 2010).

For example, as depicted in Figure 16.13, when women were shown erotic videos depicting male-male, female-female, or male-female sex, they responded *subjectively* according to their sexual preferences for male or female

Serial orgasms ▶ Repeated orgasms in women after returning directly to the plateau phase, with no intervening resolution phase (often called *multiple orgasms*).

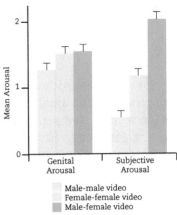

▲ **FIGURE 16.13** Heterosexual Women's Subjective and Genital Responses to Erotic Videotapes. Researcher Meredith Chivers and her colleagues found that, like men, women's reports of subjective levels of arousal were dependent upon whether the erotic videotape they were watching depicted heterosexual or homosexual activity. However, women's *genital* arousal levels were not specific to any particular category of sex. They responded to all the tapes. On the other hand, men's subjective and genital arousal almost always coincided, and the men responded only to images specific to the category of sex which they preferred.

partners. If they were *lesbian* (homosexual) they preferred the female-female images, and if *straight* (heterosexual) they preferred the male-female images. However, they experienced similar levels of *genital* arousal to *all* of the videos (Chivers, Rieger, Latty, & Bailey, 2004; Suschinsky, Lalumière, & Chivers, 2009). Indeed, in another study, Chivers found that women may even experience at least some genital arousal when watching videos of nonhuman primates engaging in sexual behavior (Chivers & Bailey, 2005).

On the other hand, in these experiments, men only responded to images reflecting their sexual orientation. Straight men responded only to the male-female or female-female images, and *gay* (homosexual) men responded only to the male-male images. Men did not respond at all to images of nonhuman primates. Moreover, unlike women, men's reported subjective arousal was consistent with their level of genital arousal. Interestingly, Chivers and her colleagues (2004) also included a sample of formerly male transsexuals who had transitioned to female identities. Their arousal patterns were identical to men's.

The research by Chivers and her colleagues suggests two important sex differences in sexual response and behavior. First, while men's subjective feelings of arousal are virtually always tied to genital sensations and arousal, the same may not always hold true for women, who may experience genital arousal when presented with sexual situations even if they experience no subjective feelings of arousal. Second, there may be a more *fluid* character to women's sexual response in general—that is, it may be less fixed on specific situations and genders and more subject to change (Diamond, 2008). Evidence to support this view will be explored later in the chapter when we discuss *sexual orientation*.

LIVING PSYCHOLOGY

Sexual Aggression: What Should You Do If You Are Raped or Sexually Assaulted?

Sexual acts committed on another person without that person's consent are termed **sexual aggression**. Such acts are the antithesis of ethical sexuality as viewed by virtually all major religions and secular moral, legal, and ethical systems. In fact, there is no other topic upon which *all* major sexual ideologies are in agreement. However, specific definitions of common acts of sexual aggression may vary considerably. For example, traditionally, *rape* was defined as vaginal sexual intercourse with a woman against her will and without her consent. However, more recently,

LIVING PSYCHOLOGY

CONTINUED

Sexual aggression ▶ Sexual acts committed on another person without that person's consent. Sexual aggression includes rape, sexual assault, and sexual abuse.

the term *rape* is often used to include crimes such as anal intercourse with a man without his consent ("male rape"), or sexual intercourse with a woman who may have appeared willing at the time, but who was unable to give true consent because she was high on drugs or alcohol ("date rape"). In general, terms such as *sexual assault* and *sexual abuse* are reserved for other types of criminal sexual acts such as nonconsensual oral sex or "groping," or any sexual interaction between an adult and a minor ("child sexual abuse").

Although published prevalence rates of sexual assault and rape are notoriously unreliable (and vary radically depending upon how these crimes are defined, who is being surveyed, and how participants are asked about their experiences), without doubt crimes of sexual aggression are prevalent in our society to a frightening degree.

What should you do if you are raped or sexually assaulted? The following set of guidelines is derived from advice given by the Coalition against Sexual Assault at Hobart and William Smith College and by similar organizations elsewhere:

1. **Make sure you are safe.** This is the first and most important thing you must do. Call 911 if you perceive yourself to be in immediate danger and are able to make the call. Go to a safe place immediately.

2. **Most rape survivor counselors suggest that you report the crime to the police, but it is your decision to make.** If there is *any* possibility that you will want to report the crime, then do not wash *any* part of your body, as difficult as this might be. Do *not* change your clothes, brush or comb your hair, or brush your teeth. Do not touch *anything* at the scene of the crime if you can avoid it. If possible—again, as difficult as this may be—try not to urinate or defecate. If there is *any* possibility you will want to make a police report, try to recall details of the perpetrator's appearance and mannerisms. Keep these details fresh in your mind by mentally rehearsing them, unless doing so is too painful.

3. **Go to a hospital or clinic.** Be prepared for a physical examination and treatment, including preventive treatment for STDs and/or pregnancy, depending on the circumstances. Some hospitals have nurses specially trained to conduct sexual assault and rape examinations. It cannot hurt to request such a nurse.

4. **Call someone you trust.** Even if they cannot truly understand how you are feeling, it is important to have the support of a person who cares about you. ■

IN SUMMARY

1. Sexual behavior is highly diverse, and people do not always agree as to what constitutes "having sex." The term *sexual behavior* itself can only be defined in circular terms.

2. Sexual fantasy is the most common form of sexual behavior. The vast majority of people fantasize at one time or another, often several times per day. Fantasy is not a substitute for sex but is often used to enhance one's sex life.

3. Men's and women's sexual response cycles are not identical. Women's cycle contains a plateau stage absent from men's, women may experience serial orgasms where men do not, women may not experience orgasm at all whereas men almost always do, and men almost always experience a refractory period after orgasm, whereas a woman may or may not wish to continue with sexual activity after orgasm.

RETRIEVE!

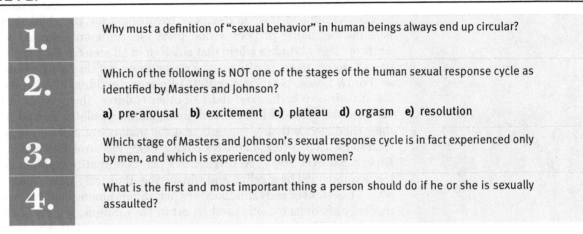

1. Why must a definition of "sexual behavior" in human beings always end up circular?

2. Which of the following is NOT one of the stages of the human sexual response cycle as identified by Masters and Johnson?

a) pre-arousal **b)** excitement **c)** plateau **d)** orgasm **e)** resolution

3. Which stage of Masters and Johnson's sexual response cycle is in fact experienced only by men, and which is experienced only by women?

4. What is the first and most important thing a person should do if he or she is sexually assaulted?

How Does Sexuality Develop?

Sexuality, like other aspects of human life, is a developmental process. It does not arrive in full force on a person's 13th, 16th, or 18th birthday, or on one's wedding night. Though it may seem odd, sexual behavior begins before birth—and may continue until the moment of death.

Child Sexuality Is Human Sexuality, but It Isn't Adult Sexuality

You might have read that "infants and children are sexual beings." But how can infants be sexual? They can't walk or talk, let alone go out on dates or run to the convenience store for condoms. When they eat, they turn their pasta dishes upside down on their heads. As they grow into toddlers, they throw tantrums in grocery stores and pick their noses. These are *not* sexually attractive characteristics. However, when psychologists say that infants and children are "sexual beings" they do not mean that sexuality of children is similar to that of adults. This is because *adult sexuality* is not synonymous with *human sexuality*, although it is often assumed to be.

Human sexual behavior begins before birth. Ultrasound images have shown that male fetuses may grasp their own genitals, and male infants have been observed to emerge from the womb with an erection. Erection in male newborn infants has been observed during nursing, during sleep, in response to manipulation, or simply spontaneously (Langfeldt, 1990; Newton & Newton, 1967). Vaginal lubrication and swelling in female infants as a consequence of exposure to maternal hormones has also been documented in the first 24

▲ **Adolescence Marks the Flowering of Adult Sexuality.**

Masturbation ▶ Pleasuring oneself through manipulation of one's own genitals.

Sex play ▶ Sexual behavior of children that is primarily exploratory or playful in nature. Children throughout the world engage in sex play, and such play appears to be generally harmless unless it is accompanied by guilt or aggression.

Primary sex characteristics ▶ Development in the reproductive and sexual organs.

hours after birth, and may also occur prior to birth (Masters, Johnson, & Kolodny, 1982). Masturbation is remarkably common in infancy (de Graaf & Rademakers, 2006; Kinsey, Pomeroy, & Martin, 1948; Kinsey, Pomeroy, Martin, & Gebhard, 1953). However, it should be understood that this is the case only if we define **masturbation** broadly as *self-stimulation of the genital area for the purpose of experiencing pleasure.* The rhythmic, repetitious manipulation of the genitals characteristic of adolescent and adult masturbation is not evident (if it appears in childhood at all) at least until the toddler reaches his or her third year, and usually well into childhood (Frayser, 1994).

The sexual life of very young children is not limited to masturbation. Just as early childhood inaugurates peer friendships for the child, it also signals the beginning of peer sexual behavior, commonly termed **sex play**. Anthropological studies affirm that children in all societies for which data exist will engage in sex play to one degree or another if they are permitted to do so (Ford & Beach, 1951; Frayser, 1994). Preschool children have great curiosity about their own bodies and those of other children, the genitals in particular (Schurke, 2000). Most research using adults' recollections and reports of their childhood activities suggests that the majority of children engage in at least some sex play (e.g., Lamb & Coakley, 1993; Vizcarral, Balladares, Candia, Lepe, & Saldivia, 2004). At this age, sex play is primarily exploratory and often accompanied by giggling and whispering, thus truly warranting the term *play*. The extent of early childhood sex play differs among cultures, as does the tendency of adults to notice and report it. For example, reports of childhood sex play in Northern European countries, such the Netherlands, Sweden, and Denmark are more widespread than in the United States (de Graaf & Rademakers, 2006; Larsson, Svedin, & Friedrich, 2000).

Is childhood sex play harmful? Although sex play often elicits anxiety in adults, there is no evidence that engaging in sex play—or refraining from it—has either beneficial or harmful consequences for children as a general rule (Friedrich, Whiteside, & Talley, 2004; Okami, Olmstead, & Abramson, 1997). According to the available research, two factors tend to be associated with unpleasant or harmful peer experiences: *aggression* and *guilt* (Friedrich et al., 2004; Haugaard & Tilly, 1988). In at least one study, adults describing childhood experiences of sex play were most likely to report that fear of being discovered by parents was the worst aspect of the experience (Reynolds, Herbenick, & Bancroft (2003).

Sexual Development in Adolescence Is Multifaceted

Adolescence has often been wrongly portrayed as the awakening of sexuality, a kind of quantum leap from a sexless childhood to adult sexual feelings. Instead, it is more a point along a continuum of sexual development that begins before birth. Yet it is a particularly important point along this continuum—the flowering of the physiology of adult sexuality.

As many of you probably have learned firsthand, the power of the surge of hormonal release that occurs around the time of maturing of the sexual organs during puberty should not be underestimated. In addition to development in the reproductive and sexual organs, known as **primary sex characteristics**, there are physical and anatomical changes in what are termed **secondary sex characteristics** because they are not directly related to the sexual and reproductive organs (see Figure 16.14).

Characteristic emotional and psychological changes related to sexuality also occur during puberty, in addition to anatomical and physiological changes. Certainly, interest in sexual and romantic behavior greatly increases. In fact, some research suggests that the single most characteristic emotional experience of daily life among adolescents is the experience of *being in love* (Collins, Welsh, & Furman, 2009; Crouter & Booth, 2006; Steinberg & Morris, 2001). Sexual feelings at this time may be both confusing and powerful.

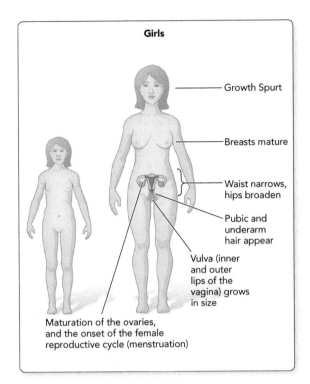 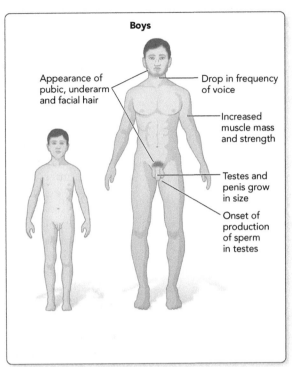

▲ **FIGURE 16.14 Primary and Secondary Sex Characteristics Appear During Puberty.** In addition to the maturation of the sexual and reproductive organs, known as *primary sex characteristics*, adolescents undergo a set of physical and anatomical changes during puberty known as secondary sex characteristics because they are not directly related to changes in reproductive and sexual organs.

"THE FIRST TIME"

What is the average age of first sexual intercourse among adolescents in the United States? This is a difficult question to answer with certainty. Statistics certainly exist, but these statistics often are derived by asking representative samples of adults or older adolescents to recall the age of their first sexual experience. But do you remember the 34-year longitudinal study of memory for events of adolescence that we discussed in Chapter 8? Seventy-three mentally healthy 14-year-old boys were interviewed about a wide range of topics (including sexuality) and then re-interviewed 34 years later at age 48. The accuracy of study participants' memory of past events was generally no better than would be expected by chance—that is, if they were guessing about someone else's responses (Offer, Kaiz, Howard, & Bennett, 2000)! If this study were alone in its findings, it might be easy to write it off as resulting from the length of the memory task (34 years) or problems with the methods used by the researchers. However, Deborah Capaldi (1996) studied a sample of adolescent boys, interviewing them annually from Grades 8 to 11. She found that responses regarding age of first intercourse were extremely unreliable.

Despite these potential problems, and noting that some figures are lower, in the United States as of 2005 almost two-thirds of U.S. adolescents have had sexual intercourse by the time they graduate from high school (Eaton et al., 2006). Apparently, much has changed in the last 50 years, either in sexual behavior or the willingness to report it (or both); during the 1950s and early 1960s, only 26% of women reported having had intercourse by age 18 (Finer, 2007; figures for men were not reported).

Socioeconomic and Ethnic Differences The figures just reported combine all ethnicities and do not distinguish groups according to income, education, and similar types of variables. However, these variables appear to make a difference. For example, in the State of West Virginia at the turn of the 21st century, 67% of women without a high school education reported having had

Secondary sex characteristics ▶ Development in anatomy and physiology which occur during puberty but are not directly related to the genitals or gonads. For example, growth of pubic and underarm hair, changes in height, breast development, changes in body shape, development of chest hair, changes in vocal pitch, and so forth.

intercourse by age 18, as compared with only 21% of college-educated women (West Virginia OMCFH, 2007); and at every age, African American teenagers (particularly males) are substantially more likely to have experienced intercourse than other ethnic groups (Abma, Martinez, Mosher, & Dawson, 2004). Extremely low-income children in the United States, interviewed over a period of 6 years in Chicago, Boston, and San Antonio, reported exceedingly young average ages of first sexual experience: The average for boys was 12.48 years and, for girls, 13.16 (total average, 12.82; Jordahl & Lohman, 2009).

On the other hand, Asian Americans and Pacific Island Americans and Canadians are unique in their reports of postponement of sexual activity in adolescence. For example, of all ethnic groups, Asian Americans and Pacific Island Americans are less likely than other adolescents to report having engaged in genital sexuality of any kind (including masturbation), and more likely to have used condoms if they had engaged in intercourse. They were also more likely to expect parental and peer disapproval if they had engaged in intercourse. In short, Asian students in North America appear to be substantially more sexually "conservative" than others on most measures of sexual behavior (Okazaki, 2002; So, Wong, & DeLeon, 2005).

Are these ethnic differences in East Asian and Pacific Island American youth genuine? Some commentators wonder if, rather than being less likely to engage in all these activities, these ethnic groups are just less likely to report them on questionnaires and in interviews. Even if this were true, however, it would still suggest an interesting ethnic difference in *attitudes* toward sexuality.

Teenage Women's Accounts How do adolescents feel about their first sexual experiences? Responses vary quite substantially, but less so for men, who fairly uniformly report positive responses to sexual initiation, at least in Western nations (Coles & Stokes, 1985; Wright et al., 2008). Indeed, initiation into sexual intercourse is almost always voluntary for men, but approximately 7% and possibly as many as 19% of sexually experienced adolescent women are pressured or overtly coerced into first intercourse. An unknown number of these coercive experiences involve forcible rape (K. A. Moore, Driscoll, & Lindberg, 1998; Wright et al., 2008). Even when acknowledging that participation was voluntary, a substantial number of young women—perhaps as many as one-third—regret their first experience of sex (Wright et al., 2008).

Although coercion and pressure unfortunately are present in many women's experiences of first intercourse, boredom and disappointment are more typical of women's accounts of their initiations into adolescent sexuality. Indeed, women often report thinking, "Is that *it*? Is that all there is to it?" (S. Thompson, 1990, 1995). However, this is far from the whole picture of sexual initiation—or later experiences—for adolescent women. The full range of responses is vividly conveyed by Sharon Thompson (1990, 1995) in her in-depth interviews with 400 female adolescents about romance and sexuality.

In interviewing adolescents, Thompson decided to focus on sex, love, romance, and pregnancy, because these topics were dominant in the thoughts and stories of her interview subjects. She asserts that descriptions of teenage women's sexual initiation fall into two basic categories of "same story." The first "same story," which we'll call "Same Story A," is highly repetitive and closely follows the stereotypical storyline of women's first experience of intercourse. Common elements are:

1. Unexpected brevity of heterosexual intercourse.

    "It was just like—psst, one minute here, the next minute it was there. It happened. That was it."

2. Pain.

    "The pain was like I couldn't stand it."

    "It felt like a knife going through me."

3. Lack of sexual knowledge.

"I had no idea. I had no idea at all. I knew I would be taking off my clothes, and I knew he'd be taking off his clothes. But as far as what would happen, I didn't know. I didn't know, you know, that a guy would put his penis in me like that, you know. I didn't know that."

4. Abdication of responsibility for the event.

"I tell you, I don't know why or how I did it. Maybe I just did it unconsciously. . . . I'm telling you, I did it unconsciously because I wouldn't do a thing like that."

5. Boredom and disappointment.

"It wasn't really that good. There was nothing I really liked about it."

"It was all right. It wasn't nothing to brag to my mother about, but it was nice."

"It wasn't that I didn't like it. It was just kind of a letdown."

▲ **Sexual Initiation in Adolescence May Occur with a Partner of the Same Sex.** The "first time" for adolescents may not necessarily consist of heterosexual intercourse. In interviews with female adolescents conducted by Sharon Thompson (1990), these teenagers sometimes reported that their first sexual experience was with another woman.

On the other hand, "Same Story B"—the second prototypical story—was told by a group Thompson refers to as "pleasure narrators." These were women who assumed that sexuality involved pleasure. They believed that "childhood sexuality and masturbation are good omens, not sins" (1990, p. 350). They discussed sex with excitement, humor, and lavish detail. Their stories of sexual pleasure "have a rich variousness that stands in eloquent contrast to the constrained, repetitive narratives . . . of pain and boredom" (pp. 350–351).

Sometimes these experiences occur with other women:

"This was the first time we ever did anything besides kiss. And I just put her down and then I touched her through her little yellow panties. She was soaked!" (1990, p. 353)

More typically, they are with same-age or somewhat older men:

"I felt good because I liked [him] and good also because I was very attracted to him and good because . . . I'd always said to myself, 'I'm not going to do it if it's the wrong time.' You know, 'I'm not going to do it when I don't want to. I'll just wait until I really want to.' And I did want to. I was glad I wanted to, and, you know, the moment was right. . . ."

IN SUMMARY

1. Self-stimulation of the genitals is nearly universal in infancy, and continues in childhood. Children in all societies, if they are permitted to, will engage in sex play to one degree or another. Sex play appears to be generally harmless unless it is accompanied by guilt or coercion.

2. Adolescence does not mark the awakening of sexuality, but it is a particularly important point along a continuum of sexual development beginning before birth. Characteristic changes include the development of primary and secondary sex characteristics as well as emotional and psychological changes.

3. Approximately 54% of U.S. women and 60% of U.S. men have had sexual intercourse by age 18. This is a substantial increase over figures collected during the 1950s and 1960s.

4. Teenage women tend to report either of two types of responses to their initiation into sexuality. The first type of response stresses feelings of boredom, pain, lack of sexual knowledge, abdication of responsibility, and disappointment. The second type stresses pleasure, humor, and excitement.

RETRIEVE!

1. True or false: Masturbation does not begin until the years just prior to the onset of puberty.

2. What are the differences between primary and secondary sex characteristics?

3. Which of the following is NOT among the elements in the accounts of sexual initiation given to interviewer Sharon Thompson and characterized as "Same Story A":

a) boredom and disappointment
b) guilt
c) lack of sexual knowledge
d) unexpected brevity of sex
e) abdication of responsibility

4. Why might reports of less (and later) sexual activity among Asian-American teenagers be inaccurate?

What Is Sexual Orientation?

Heterosexual (straight) ▶ The term used to describe a primary sexual preference for members of the other sex.

Homosexual (gay or lesbian) ▶ The term used to describe a primary sexual preference for members of one's own sex.

Bisexual (bi) ▶ The term used to describe a sexual orientation marked by varying degrees of attraction to both sexes.

What is the meaning of the term *sexual orientation*? In the past, sexual orientation was usually defined according to a general erotic attraction to the body characteristics (particularly genital characteristics) either of one's own or the other sex. Those attracted to the other sex were referred to as **heterosexual** (*straight*), those attracted to their own sex, as **homosexual** (*gay* or *lesbian*), and those attracted to both sexes as **bisexual** (*bi;* e.g., Freund, 1974).

However, this definition of sexual orientation is outdated and inadequate for a number of reasons. First, if you recall, although the large majority of human beings are unambiguously male or female, these designations do not describe *all* people. Take Jackie, a 26-year-old genetically male transgender from the Dominican Republic who lives as a female and identifies as a female. She prefers women as partners. Is she lesbian or straight? Or PJ—he's a 17-year-old *hustler* (male prostitute) on Manhattan's West Side who engages in 200 homosexual sex acts for every one or two heterosexual acts. Is he gay? What if he claims he only has sex with men for the money, but that he prefers women and labels himself straight? Or Durga, a 48-year-old college professor who strongly prefers sex with other women but also enjoys sex with men on some occasions. Is she bisexual—or a lesbian who sometimes has sex with men?

Complicating matters even further are data from sex surveys which suggest that substantial numbers of Americans who consider themselves heterosexual have had at least some homosexual experience or attraction to a person of the same sex (e.g., Kinsey et al., 1948; Kinsey et al., 1953). For example, although only 1% to 2% of women and 2% to 3% of sexually active men engage in sex exclusively with those of the same sex and/or label themselves *gay* or *lesbian*, at least 11.2% of women and 6% of men between ages 15 and 44 have had at least one sexual experience with a member of the same sex (Smith, 2006), and a total of 8% of Americans report having had at least some same-sex attraction (Laumann et al., 1994). Largely similar results have been found in studies in France and the United Kingdom (Savin-Williams & Ream, 2007).

Sexual Orientation Includes Behavior, Desire, and Identity

As you can see, things often get complicated when you try to put labels on sexual behaviors and preferences and try to define **sexual orientation**. One way of sorting out these problems is to separate sexual orientation into three areas: *behavior, desire,* and *identity* (Laumann et al., 1994). A person may fall into gay, straight, or bisexual categories on any or all of these dimensions. *Behavior* describes the sex of the persons with whom one actually engages in sexual activity. *Desire* refers to the sex of persons about whom one fantasizes and with whom one would most look forward to having sex. Sexual *identity* is the label one chooses to apply to one's sexual self, such as gay, straight, or bi. Thus, the hustler described earlier might be gay in behavior but straight in desire and identity. The professor described earlier might be bisexual in behavior and identity, but primarily lesbian in desire. This way of looking at sexual orientation might be called for convenience the *three-factor model* of sexual orientation.

On the other hand, because *desire* is probably the "engine" driving most sexual behavior—and it is perhaps the most interesting and enduring aspect of sexual choices—sexual orientation could be defined as an enduring *erotic* (i.e., sexual and/or romantic) desire for members either of one's own sex, the other sex, or both—*regardless* of the actual sex of persons with whom one engages in sexual acts, and regardless of the labels one might wish to apply to oneself or one's behavior (Savin-Williams, 2006). This could be called the *desire-driven* model of sexual orientation. According to this idea, a person might choose to label himself straight and yet actually be gay.

However, like the three-factor model, the desire-driven model is far from acceptable to everyone, and some believe that the categories *gay, straight,* and *bisexual* do not adequately capture human sexual orientation at all, regardless of how they are employed (Diamond, 2005, 2008). Instead, these theorists conceive of sexual orientation as a continuous dimension—a *continuum*—where a person can vary in the extent to which he or she experiences same-sex and other-sex desires and behaviors (Dunne, Bailey, Kirk, & Martin, 2000; see Figure 16.15). This could be referred to as the *continuum model*.

Patterns of Sexual Orientation Differ for Men and Women

Until recently there has been a general tendency to discuss sexual orientation as though it pertained identically to men and women. However, models that describe the development of nonheterosexual orientations (gay, lesbian, bisexual) were traditionally drawn from research conducted primarily among men. Yet, as we have already seen, male and female sexualities are not identical in certain respects, and this includes typical patterns of male and female sexual orientation.

Researcher Lisa Diamond conducted the first longitudinal study of the development of sexual orientation in female adolescents and young adult women (e.g., Diamond, 2000a, 2000b, 2005, 2008). Her findings challenge much conventional wisdom about homosexuality and bisexuality in women, particularly when these findings are added to data collected in national surveys and studies of genetic influences on sexual orientation.

For example, take another look at the graph in Figure 16.15 based on research on a nationally representative U.S. sample by Edward Laumann and his colleagues (1994). The pattern appears quite similar for men and women until one arrives at the "only same sex" category at the far right of the graph. Substantially more men than women are interested *only* in same-sex partners—that is, women's "nonheterosexuality" is spread out more evenly among those who prefer only same-sex partners and those with varying

▲ **Sexual orientation includes behavior, desire, and identity.** Sexual orientation is a complex aspect of human sexuality. It incorporates *behavior* (the actual sex of your partner); *desire* (the sex of those you would prefer to have sex with, or about whom you fantasize); and *identity* (which sexual orientation you consider yourself to have).

Sexual orientation ▶ A complex term that is defined differently by different people. The *three-factor* model takes into account (a) the sex of the people with whom one most desires to have sex; (b) the sex of the people with whom one actually has sex; and (c) the label one chooses to apply to one's sexual identity (gay, straight, or bisexual). The *desire-driven* model defines sexual orientation as "an enduring erotic desire for members either of one's own sex, the other sex, or both— regardless of the actual sex of the persons with whom one engages in sex and regardless of the label one used to apply to oneself." The *continuum* model suggests that categories like *gay, straight,* and *bisexual* cannot adequately capture sexual orientation at all—proposing instead that people can vary greatly in the extent to which they experience same-sex and other-sex desires and behaviors.

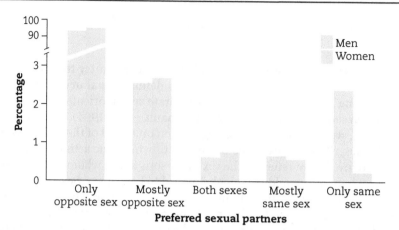

▲ **FIGURE 16.15   A Continuum of Sexual Orientations?** Data collected in the United States by Laumann et al. (1994) shows that, while the vast majority of people express a sexual interest only in those of the other sex, some express an interest only in those of the same sex and some express *varying degrees* of interest in those of the same and other sex. Should *all* those who express *any* interest in members of the same sex be considered "bisexual"—even if they are "mostly" attracted to members of the *other* sex? Because an interest "mostly in the other sex" seems qualitatively different from an interest "mostly in the same sex," which also differs from a more or less equal interest in both sexes, some have argued that a continuum model of sexual orientation might best describe the data—a model that allows one person to be more or less gay or straight than another person. Other theorists insist that "mostly" is so close to "only" as to be essentially indistinguishable—ending up with the traditional three-point category system *gay*, *straight*, and *bi*. (Source: LeVay & Valente, 2003, p. 201.)

degrees of interest in both sexes (see also Bailey, Dunne, & Martin, 2000; Smith, 2006).

In another study, which included a sample of almost 200,000 men and women from 15 nations on four continents conducted via the Internet, Richard Lippa (2006; 2007) showed that women who reported higher sex drives (motivation to engage in sex) also reported a greater likelihood of being at least somewhat attracted to both men and women. On the other hand, men reporting higher sex drives were much more likely to report being attracted *only* to other men *or* to women, depending on their stated sexual preference. Taken together, these results suggest that men are more "fixed" in their sexual preferences.

Why should men and women differ in these ways? Lisa Diamond's research may help to clarify the statistics reported in the previous two paragraphs. Her research shows that women's sexual orientation is more "fluid" and subject to change over time than men's, and less easy to characterize using only the labels *lesbian, straight,* and *bisexual.* While some women adopt a stable and consistent lesbian identity early in life—similar to the pattern for gay men—others move from one sexual identity to another over time. This may happen when a woman finds herself falling in love with a person of the sex other than that to which she previously had been attracted. Such a woman may adopt a new sexual identity and remain there, or shift back and forth between lesbian and straight identities throughout her life, depending upon her relationships (E. M. Thompson & Morgan, 2008). Others in similar situations may adopt a bisexual identity or refuse to label themselves at all. Indeed, of all the patterns of non-heterosexuality among women observed by Diamond, *stable lesbians*—who show no sexual interest in men throughout their lives—constitute the "smallest, least representative" group (2000b, p. 300). On the other hand, stable homosexuality is the rule among gay men.

Causes of Sexual Orientation Are Not Known with Certainty

Treating gay men and lesbians as persons with a "condition" that has a cause—much like a disease—has a long and unfortunate history (LeVay, 1996). Indeed, until quite recently, homosexuality was considered a mental illness in the United States and Europe, despite the fact that no evidence has ever existed that homosexuality is anything but an ordinary variant of human sexuality. Consequently—again, until relatively recently—researchers have primarily been interested in negative attributes of gay men and lesbians (Savin-Williams, 2008).

However, same-sex behavior is present in a great many, if not most, societies throughout the world (Ford & Beach, 1951), and many nonhuman animals also engage in same-sex sexual behavior (Paoli, Palagi, Tacconi, & Tarli, 2006; Sommer & Vassey, 2006). Therefore, contemporary researchers often frame their work as a search for the cause of sexual orientation in general rather than a cause of same-sex behavior or homosexual identity in particular. And yet, because exclusive or primary preference for one's own sex is still quite rare when the world's population is considered as a whole (Savin-Williams & Ream, 2007), from a scientific perspective its cause remains the more interesting.

BIOLOGY OF HOMOSEXUALITY

Early theorists of homosexuality believed that gay and lesbian identities were the result of defective parental personalities or child-rearing styles, traumatic childhood events, and other variables related to personal experiences and socialization. Because most such early theories have been discredited or abandoned for lack of evidence, current research has shifted its emphasis to biological factors, and there are a host of interesting new findings regarding neural, hormonal, anatomical, and genetic *correlates* of gay and lesbian sexual orientations (Rahman, 2005b). As described in Chapter 1, a **correlate** is any factor or variable that co-occurs with another variable, in this case, gay or lesbian sexual identity. However, *correlates* of gay and lesbian sexual orientations are not necessarily *causes*.

For example, research suggests that the size of certain structures in the brain may differ between gay and straight men, with gay men showing structural sizes and functions more commonly found in women (e.g., Byne et al., 2001; LeVay, 1991; Savic & Lindström, 2008; Witelson et al., 2008; see Table 16.4). However, even if differences in brain structures were found between all gay and straight men—and this is highly unlikely—we would still not know if such differences are a cause of homosexuality or if homosexuality over time causes changes in the size of structures in the brain. It is also possible that some unknown third variable—for example, early experiences of gender identity development—is a cause of both the brain differences *and* homosexuality.

Another important point to bear in mind is that even if *all* the biological "markers" summarized in Table 16.4 were causally related to homosexuality, evidence suggests that they would only slightly increase the odds of a person developing a gay identity, and it would be impossible to predict whether a person will be gay or straight merely because he or she shows one or more of these markers. For example, another correlate of gay male (but not lesbian) identity is the simple fact of having older, biologically related brothers (i.e., not step-brothers). The more older brothers a man has, the more likely he will be to have a gay sexual orientation[2] (Blanchard, 2008; Bogaert, 2006; Camperio-Ciani, Corna, & Capiluppi, 2004). But it is still highly unlikely that *any* given person with older brothers is gay, simply because being gay is relatively rare, while older brothers are not! It only means that with each older

▲ **Women's Sexual Orientation Patterns Are More Varied and Fluid than Men's.** Although some women with same-sex orientations label themselves "lesbian," others adopt a bisexual identity or refuse to label themselves at all. Pictured here is a female couple from South Africa, the first African nation to permit gay and lesbian marriage.

Correlate ▶ Any factor or variable that co-occurs with some other variable.

---

[2] *Conflicting research suggests that this may hold true only for right-handed men!*

Table 16.4 Some Biological Correlates (Markers) of Gay Sexual Identity in Men

Note: *These findings require replication before they are fully accepted.*

Brain Structure
INAH3, a nucleus of the hypothalamus, is somewhat *smaller* in gay than straight men and more similar in size to that found in women (Byne et al., 2001; LeVay, 1991).
Fibers connecting the right and left hemispheres of the cerebral cortex are somewhat *larger* in gay men than straight men and more similar in size to that found in straight women (Allen & Gorski, 1992).
Isthmus area of the corpus callosum is *larger* in gay men (Witelson et al., 2008).
Cerebral hemispheres symmetrical in straight women and gay men, but right hemispheres slightly larger in gay women and straight men. Patterns of connections between certain brain structures also differ between gay and straight research participants (PET and fMRI study; Savic & Lindström, 2008).

Male Siblings
The greater the number of older (genetically related) brothers, the more likely a man is to develop gay sexual orientation (Bogaert, 2006; Camperio-Ciani et al., 2004).

Anatomy
Gay men are more likely than straight men to be left-handed or both-handed (ambidextrous; Blanchard, Cantor, Bogaert, Breedlove et al., 2006).
Gay men have fewer fingerprint ridges on the right hand relative to the left (Mustanski, Bailey, & Kaspar, 2002).
Gay men have a shorter ratio of the second to fourth finger than the average heterosexual man (2D/4D), a likely marker of prenatal hormone exposure (Rahman, 2005a).

Genetic
Identical (monozygotic) twins are far more likely than nontwins or fraternal (dizygotic) twins to share their sexual orientation. Approximately 20% to 37% of members of an identical twin pair who is gay or lesbian have a twin who is also gay or lesbian (Bailey et al., 2000; Kendler et al., 2000).

brother the likelihood of a man developing gay sexual identity increases—if only to a relatively small degree.

What about lesbians? There are fewer such biological markers of sexual orientation for lesbians, perhaps because, in keeping with research described earlier, non-heterosexuality among women is more varied as to type and perhaps also more varied as to cause (e.g., Langström, Rahman, Carlström, & Lichtenstein, 2008). If women are more likely than men to follow a continuum model of sexual orientation—with greater variability in their degrees of attraction to the same and other sex—it may be less likely that reliable biological markers will ever be found.

Finally, as discussed in detail in Chapters 3, 9, and 12, there is genetic influence on the expression of most traits in human beings, and sexual orientation is no exception (Dawood, Bailey, & Martin, 2009). Like the personality characteristics discussed in Chapter 12, both male and female identical twins are much more likely than nontwin or fraternal twin siblings to share a sexual orientation. However, although many *more* identical twins than other siblings share their sexual orientation, this does not mean that *most* do. In fact, at least two-thirds of gay or lesbian members of an identical twin pair do *not* have a twin who is also gay or lesbian (Bailey et al., 2000; Kendler, Thornton,

Gilman, & Kessler, 2000; Langström et al., 2008). As with other biological markers, genetics cannot tell the whole story of sexual orientation. Indeed, pathways to sexual orientation are likely to differ among different people. We may use the term *homosexuality* for convenience, but we are more accurately speaking of *homosexualities*.

IN SUMMARY

1. Sexual orientation includes factors related to desire, behavior, and identity. Definitions of sexual orientation are controversial.

2. Patterns of sexual orientation differ for men and women. Women's sexual orientation appears to be more fluid—more subject to change over time.

3. Causes of sexual orientation are not known with certainty. Because exclusive preference for members of one's own sex is rare, most research in sexual orientation development has focused on causes of homosexuality. Early theories of homosexual development which stressed relationships with parents or traumatic childhood experiences have largely been abandoned, and research emphasis has shifted to biological factors. But these factors are merely correlates and do not predict homosexuality in any given individual.

RETRIEVE!

1. Explain the difference between desire, identity, and behavior in sexual orientation.

2. What is the continuum model of sexual orientation? What statistical evidence, presented in a graph in the chapter, supports this model? Contrast this model with the *desire-driven* and *three-factor* models of sexual orientation.

3. Name at least three ways in which female homosexuality differs from male homosexuality.

4. Name at least three biological markers (correlates) of male homosexuality.

5. True or false: If one identical twin is gay or lesbian, the other twin is highly likely also to be gay or lesbian.

How Closely Are Sex and Love Linked?

As many teenagers have been warned by their parents, love and sexual desire are not the same—even though it might sometimes feel as though they are, and we can grant that they do often occur together. Researchers have recently taken seriously the challenge of determining just how love and sex are linked—or not linked (Aron, Fisher, Mashek, Strong, & Brown, 2005; Diamond, 2008; Gonzaga, Turner, Keltner, Campos, & Altemus, 2006; Hatfield & Rapson, 2005). Before considering this question, however, we need to *define our*

▲ Cross-Species Love? When Bella, a dog, suffered a spinal cord injury, her friend and constant companion, an elephant named Tarra, held vigil for 3 weeks while the dog lay motionless up in the Elephant Sanctuary's office. With 2,700 acres to roam free, Tarra just stood in the corner beside a gate outside the office until Bella was healed. That event, and this photo, certainly does appear to express something remarkably similar to what might be called "love" in a human being. However, making such assumptions is an example of anthropomorphizing—rightly or wrongly attributing human qualities to nonhumans. *(Source: Phillips, 2008.)*

variables. We've spent the chapter discussing sex, and we now know what we mean when we use the word. What about love?

Love as a Set of Characteristic Feelings, Thoughts, and Behaviors

What *is* love? I must confess that I cannot answer this question. What compounds the problem is that the word *love* is used casually in contexts that differ so radically that it is difficult even to conceive of *love* as referring to any specific condition or emotion (Berscheid, 2010; Reis & Aron, 2008). For example, I love my wife, my children, and my cats. But I also love really good sushi and pizza (not eaten together, though). I love jazz musicians Thelonious Monk and Clifford Brown, the New Mexico sky at night, Japanese architecture and martial arts, and Brazilian Portuguese spoken with a Rio de Janeiro accent. If pressed, I will have to be honest and admit that I also "love" Scarlett Johannsen in *The Girl with a Pearl Earring* (but don't tell my wife). How can one word be used to describe all of this?

Although you can love a movie performance, a food, the sky, or a language accent, let us narrow the term *love* down to refer only to feelings a human being has about another entity in the context of a relationship—and by *entity* we are including not only another person, but also a pet or even a deity (Reis & Aron, 2008). This will make it at least conceivably possible to have a discussion about love within the space my publisher has allotted! However, even love between persons and entities comes in a great many forms; from *agape* (spiritual, selfless love, as in love of one's children, one's God, or humanity itself) to *platonic love* (friendship), *manic* or *obsessive love*, *romantic love*, and numerous other styles of love (Hendrick & Hendrick, 2006; Lee, 1976).

Yet what is usually on people's minds—at least young people's minds—when they think of *love* is *romantic love*, sometimes also termed *passionate love* (Hatfield & Rapson, 2005; Lieberman & Hatfield, 2006). This is the sort of love that tends to co-occur with sexuality. We will examine love in two ways: as a set of feelings, thoughts, and behaviors; and as a universal human experience with many cultural variations. We shall then look at the connections—and disconnections—between love and sex.

> *"My whole world had been transformed. It had a new center, and that center was Marilyn."*

> —Man in love (cited by Fisher, 2004, p. 6)

Some psychologists consider love to be an emotion by itself—even a basic emotion as described in Chapter 11 (e.g., Shaver, Morgan, & Wu, 1996). However, because there is no particular facial expression or specific body language associated with love, and because of love's complexity and contradictions, most theorists probably view love (at least romantic love) as a collection of different emotions, motivations, goal-directed behaviors, and cognitions (e.g., Aron et al., 2005; Reis & Aron, 2008). Exactly what these emotions, motivations, and behaviors are, however, is not agreed upon.

In her study of the biochemistry and evolutionary psychology of passionate (romantic) love, evolutionary psychologist Helen Fisher (2004, pp. 6–24) lists a set of 20 emotional-motivational, cognitive, and behavioral characteristics of the experience of being "in love," and this seems a good place to start. Briefly summarizing just a few of these characteristics, when a couple is in love:

- The beloved becomes unique and all important—all your attention is focused upon him or her, frequently to the detriment of everything and everyone else around you.
- The beloved's failings are greatly minimized, and his or her good qualities exaggerated.

- It is very difficult to stop thinking about the beloved—thoughts of him or her are obsessive and intrusive.
- A person in love is beset by frequent mood swings.
- Lovers might find themselves changing clothing style, mannerisms, habits, taste in music, and even values to win their beloved.
- Those in love become highly dependent upon the relationship, and feelings of sexual passion and jealousy are generally ignited.

Unfortunately—or fortunately, depending on your point of view—research has repeatedly shown that feelings of passionate love are temporary, and the sorts of experiences just described rarely last more than a year or two, according to researchers in the neurobiology of love (Emanuele et al., 2006; Marazziti, Akiskal, Rossi, & Cassano, 1999; Marazziti & Canale, 2004). However, Fisher herself thinks the actual length of time can be longer—particularly if there is some type of adversity or barrier to the union fanning the flames. Indeed, as Romeo and Juliet quickly discovered, the experience of adversity can play a large part in the flowering and maintenance of romantic love.

> "I know true love exists. I just can't prove it."
>
> —David Buss, evolutionary psychologist

Love Is a Human Universal—With Cultural Variations

It was popular among psychologists some years back to assert that romantic love was a "social construction" and that it did not exist prior to the 19th-century era of romanticism (or, for some, the 14th-century era of chivalry). These commentators also tended to assert that romantic love could only exist in Western societies. But in fact, the unique union of intimacy and passion we refer to as romantic love appears to be present in virtually all human societies for which adequate information is available, and also appears to have existed throughout history—as a simple review of world literature across the ages will attest (Hatfield & Rapson, 2005; Jankowiak & Fisher, 1992; Reis & Aron, 2008).

Consider the following intimate dialogue between two teenagers from the mountains of central India, as recorded by an ethnographer of the region:

> "All day you were in my eyes," says the boy. "You went to that village, and I kept on looking at it and saying to myself, 'She is there.'"
>
> "Yes, I went away," responds the girl, "but I felt as if you were just behind me. I could see your shadow by me all the time."
>
> "All day long I felt as if you were actually talking to me."
>
> "I said to myself, 'Now the sun stands overhead; he must have returned from the jungle with his wood; perhaps he is resting, perhaps he is drinking his *jawa*.'"
>
> "I felt as if I should take you away, and talk to you alone, and never hear anyone else's voice again."
>
> "I never want to hear anyone else either. . . ." (Elwin, 1968, pp. 126–127)

Though you may live closer to central Detroit than to the mountains of central India, we suspect that at least some of you have felt as these lovers do, or spoken similar words—translated to your own cultural setting.

However, love *is* constructed somewhat differently in each society—in the importance individuals place upon it, its general prevalence, associated rituals, beliefs about its typical outcome, and the degree to which it is permitted to flourish (Endleman, 1989; Gregor, 1995; Hatfield & Rapson, 2005; Levine, Sato, Hashimoto, & Verma, 1995). Culture helps determine when, with whom, and how we fall in love (Lieberman & Hatfield, 2006).

One example of the important influence of culture on romantic love emerges from comparisons between Western societies, such as the United States and (Southern) Europe, and Chinese society. In Western societies falling in love is usually equated with happiness, and this view is reflected in much of Western poetry and popular music (Shaver, Wu, & Schwartz, 1992). Public displays of romantic love are usually tolerated, or even looked upon with amused appreciation.

On the other hand, in China, public displays of love are strongly frowned upon, and romantic love is more often associated with sorrow, sometimes considered more of an unfortunate affliction than a blessing. This might be thought somewhat reminiscent of medieval European courtly images of love, in which suffering and longing follow unrequited love or separation of lovers due to social circumstances such as war, family feuds, and social status.

Fred Rothbaum and Bill Yuk-Piu Tsang (1998) conducted an analysis of the content of approximately 40 popular songs from China and 40 from the United States, looking for reflections of cultural differences in the nature of romantic love in the two societies. In addition to differences in the association of love with happiness or sadness, they found that love is much more *embedded*, or absorbed, into other aspects of life within Chinese society than in the United States and therefore appears to play a less important role among Chinese people. As Hsu wrote, "An American asks, 'How does my heart feel?' A Chinese asks, 'What will other people say?'" (cited by Hatfield & Rapson, 2005, p. 16). Nonetheless, when romantic love occurs among Chinese people, it is experienced with an intensity equivalent to that found among Westerners (Doherty, Hatfield, Thompson, & Choo, 1994; Rothbaum & Tsang, 1998).

Cultural differences in the importance placed on romantic love are also reflected in a survey of citizens of 11 nations on five continents (Levine et al., 1995). Levine and colleagues asked the question: "If a man (woman) had all the other qualities you desired, would you marry this person if you were not in love with him (her)?" As shown in Table 16.5, of the 11 nations, U.S. citizens were the most likely to answer "No."

Despite cultural differences, however, the quality and expressions of romantic love are far more similar among cultures than different (Hatfield & Rapson, 2005; Lieberman & Hatfield, 2006; Sprecher et al., 1994). Thus, cross-cultural comparisons, while pointing out often profound qualitative differences, constitute the best evidence we have of the universal potential for romantic love among human beings.

Love and Sex: The Biobehavioral Model

Now that we have taken a stab at defining romantic love by looking at its characteristics, let us look at current research and theory on the connections—and disconnections—between love and sex. Lisa Diamond, whose work on female

Table 16.5 "Would You Marry without Being in Love?" Asked in 11 Cultures

Responses to Question 1: "If a man (woman) had all the other qualities you desired, would you marry this person if you were not in love with him (her)?"

RESPONSE	INDIA	PAKISTAN	THAILAND	UNITED STATES	ENGLAND	JAPAN	PHILIPPINES	MEXICO	BRAZIL	HONG KONG	AUSTRALIA
Yes	49.0	50.4	18.8	3.5	7.3	2.3	11.4	10.2	4.3	5.8	4.8
No	24.0	39.1	33.8	85.9	83.6	62.0	63.6	80.5	85.7	77.6	80.0
Undecided	26.9	10.4	47.5	10.6	9.1	35.7	25.0	9.3	10.0	16.7	15.2

NOTE: Figures given are in percentages. (*Source: Levine et al. 1995.*)

sexual orientation we reviewed earlier, has generated a model of the relationship between romantic love and sexual desire which combines findings from neurohormonal, sociocultural, and evolutionary psychology research. She terms it the *biobehavioral model* of romantic love and sexual desire (Diamond, 2003, 2004, 2008).

Diamond begins by pointing out that most people could imagine sexual desire without romantic love, but fewer could image romantic love without sexual desire. Yet such experiences exist—consider a young child's infatuation with a teacher or another child, or the voluminous historical reports of gay or straight people astonished to find themselves developing intense feelings of attachment, intimacy, and longing for another person—that is, romantic love—even though that person is of the "wrong sex." In such cases, overt feelings of passion or sexual attraction may sometimes be relatively or entirely absent (evidence summarized in Diamond, 2003, 2008).

According to Diamond, sex and love may become disconnected because romantic and sexual feelings have different neural and hormonal components and distinct evolutionary histories. As she points out, the sex hormones estrogen and testosterone are the primary neurobiological systems governing sexual desire (Wallen, 2001), but they are not implicated at all in the forming of affectional bonds. Instead, the feelings associated with bonding and affectionate attachments appear to be linked to the various reward centers of the brain and the chemicals which fluctuate within these centers, including endorphins and the neurotransmitters dopamine and oxytocin (which also functions as a hormone; Aron et al., 2005).

There is also an evolutionary component to the biological "disconnect" between love and sex, according to Diamond. Theorists such as John Bowlby, the originator of attachment theory as described in Chapter 4, have proposed that the human capacity to form close attachments and affectionate bonding evolved to promote behaviors which kept infants in close proximity to their caregivers, maximizing the infants' chances of survival. Infant-caretaker bonds create feelings of comfort and security between the pair during times together, and feelings of anxiety and distress upon separation.

Does that sound like the way people feel when they are deeply in love? There may be a good reason for the similarity. Diamond proposes that over evolutionary time, mechanisms which originally evolved to promote infant-caregiver attachment came to serve a second purpose. This second purpose is keeping parents together for the purpose of rearing their offspring to maturity—in other words, adult pair-bonding through romantic love. Thus, sexual desire evolved to serve a *reproductive* function, while romantic love evolved to serve a *commitment* function (Gonzaga et al., 2006; Hazan & Zeifman, 1999).

DOES RESEARCH SUPPORT THE BIOBEHAVIORAL MODEL?

Much of Diamond's theory is speculative, but some recent research offers evidence consistent with it. Gian Gonzaga and his colleagues videotaped a multiethnic sample of young monogamous couples as they discussed various topics that had been given them by the investigators (Gonzaga et al., 2006). One of these topics was the couple's first date—a discussion with the potential to elicit both feelings of love and feelings of desire. Later, the couples filled out detailed reports about their feelings during the discussion.

Without knowledge of how the couples had filled out the reports, from the videos Gonzaga and his research team coded the body language, movements, gestures, and facial expressions of each couple during the first-date discussion. The researchers identified various behaviors known from previous research to be associated with personal reports of feelings either of love or sexual desire, but not both.

For example, feelings of love are associated with (among other things) the natural ("Duchenne") smile described in Chapter 10, affirmative nods of the head, leaning toward the partner, and positive hand gestures. Sexual desire is

▶**FIGURE 16.16** Romantic Love and Maternal Love Overlap in Oxytocin-Rich Regions of the Brain. In a series of studies of the expression of romantic and maternal love, Bartels and Zeki (2000, 2004) found that maternal love and romantic love—while activating certain brain regions independently—also activate overlapping regions. In the top figure (1A, B, C, D), areas of the brain activated while women viewed photographs of their own children (but not activated while viewing others' children) are shown in yellow. Areas activated when men and women viewed images of their spouses or lovers (but not when viewing images of friends) are shown in red. Areas where activation for feelings of maternal and romantic love overlaps appear orange-colored. These areas are rich in oxytocin receptors.

The bottom figure shows that areas of the brain *de*activated during maternal love are markedly similar to those deactivated during romantic love. These areas are known to be activated during the experience of negative emotions and when passing critical judgments on others.

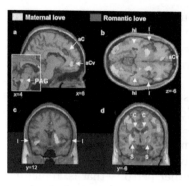

1a, b, c, d)   ACTIVATION

Abbreviations code:
aC = anterior cingulated cortex
aCv = ventral aC
C = caudate nucleus
F = frontal eye fields
Fu = - fusiform cortex
I = insula
S = striatum
PAG = periaqueductal gray
Hi = hippocampus

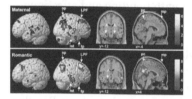

DEACTIVATION

Abbreviations code:
op = ocipitoparietal junction
LPF = lateral prefrontal cortex
mt = middle temporal cortex
tp = temporal pole
A = Amygdaloid cortex
pc = posterior cingulated cortex
mp = mesial prefrontal/paracingulate gyrus

associated with gestures such as lip licking or puckering, touching the lips, and protrusion of the tongue. The researchers found that the extent to which they observed "love-cues" such as these on the videotapes was associated with the degree to which the couple reported that they were feeling love at the time, and the extent to which "desire-cues" were observed was associated with feelings of desire. These findings show that while love and desire can overlap, they do not necessarily do so.

In a separate study reported in the same article, Gonzaga and his colleagues turned to the neurohormonal basis of romantic love. They induced a sample of women to mentally relive an experience of romantic love or infatuation. As the women did so, they were videotaped and blood samples were repeatedly drawn. The investigators found that oxytocin release was associated with the appearance of "love cues" (e.g., natural smile) but not "desire cues" (e.g., lip licking).

Andreas Bartels and Semir Zeki (2000, 2004) used fMRI brain imaging technology to provide even more vivid evidence of the role of oxytocin, the relationship between feelings of romantic love and reward centers of the brain, and the evolutionary connection between maternal love and romantic love. As depicted in Figure 16.16, although regions of the brain activated while experiencing feelings of maternal love differ in certain respects from those activated during feelings of romantic love, the two also overlap in numerous regions. These overlapping areas are rich in oxytocin receptors. Moreover, areas of the brain associated with negative emotions and critical judgments of others are virtually identically *de*activated for both maternal and romantic love.

Although these research findings are consistent with Diamond's biobehavioral theory of romantic love and sexual desire, it is important to point out that research findings *consistent* with a theory do not necessarily demonstrate that the theory is *true*. For example, consider the findings that areas of the brain associated with negative emotion and critical judgments of others are deactivated both for maternal and romantic love. This does not prove a unique connection between maternal and romantic love—these brain regions may become deactivated during any number of positive emotional experiences. Unless other such experiences are controlled for, we cannot be certain that a unique link between maternal and romantic love exists in these brain regions. Thus, it will take a substantial number of replications—using a variety of research methods—before a theory with implications as far-reaching as Diamond's can be fully accepted.

IN SUMMARY

1. Although some psychologists view love as an emotion, most view love as a collection of different emotions, motivations, goal-directed behaviors, and cognitions.

2. Helen Fisher has compiled a set of 20 emotional, cognitive, and behavioral characteristics of the experience of being "in love." Although love may last a lifetime, being "in love" rarely lasts longer than 1 to 2 years.

3. Romantic love is a human universal. However, love differs in each society in the importance individuals place upon it, its general prevalence, associated rituals, beliefs about its typical outcome, and the degree to which it is permitted to flourish.

4. Lisa Diamond's biobehavioral theory of romantic love and sexual desire states that love and desire have different neurohormonal components and evolutionary histories. Thus, while desire and love are often linked, each can also exist without the other. Diamond's theory is speculative, but some research is consistent with it. Nevertheless, some of the research findings may be explained in ways other than those predicted by the theory.

RETRIEVE!

1. List at least three of the emotional, cognitive, or behavioral characteristics of being "in love" as described by Helen Fisher.

2. What is one important difference between the way that romantic love is viewed in the United States and in China?

3. Sexual desire is governed primarily by the sex hormones _____ and _____.

    a) estrogen/testosterone   **c)** oxytocin/dopamine

    b) progesterone/testosterone   **d)** estrogen/oxytocin

4. Experiences of bonding and attachment are governed primarily by the neurotransmitters _____ and _____.

    a) estrogen/testosterone   **c)** oxytocin/dopamine

    b) progesterone/testosterone   **d)** estrogen/oxytocin

5. What is the evolutionary origin of romantic love, according to Lisa Diamond's theory?

Looking Back

Chapter 16 in Review

ARE "SEX" AND "GENDER" DIFFERENT?

- Human sexuality includes sex, gender, and sexual behavior. Determining sex at birth includes chromosomal, gonadal, hormonal, and anatomical factors. To be born female (XX), an individual must inherit two X chromosomes, one from each parent. To be born male (XY), the individual must inherit one X and one Y chromosome. The gonad is the reproductive organ—testes in males, ovaries in females. If the fertilizing sperm is Y-bearing, the SRY gene triggers the creation of proteins that develop into the male gonad. Otherwise, the fetus develops female gonads. The hormonal balance of the fetus is the balance between estrogen and testosterone. Anatomical sex is the actual development of male or female genitals.

- Chromosomes, fetal gonads, hormonal balance and anatomy usually coincide to produce infants who are unambiguously male or female. Intersex refers to individuals born with the appearance of genitals opposite to their chromosomal sex, or with aspects of both male and female gonads and genital tissue.

- "Gender" is harder to define than "sex." Gender identity refers to people's subjective perception of the sex they belong to or identify with. The term "gender" has been used more broadly to promote the view that sex roles and sex differences are actually social and psychological categories, and the term "sex" has been used more narrowly to refer to physical anatomy. However, there are numerous problems with dividing sexuality into "sex" and "gender."

- Gender identity begins in toddlerhood. Gender schema theory holds that toddlers acquire schemas about gender that summarize the child's interpretations of information about gender. Once acquired,

Looking Back continued

the schema controls the way the toddler attends and responds to new information. Evolutionary theorists propose that human beings have evolved a preverbal level of understanding about gender that emerges much earlier than the third year.

- Transsexual describes a person who identifies with the sex other than the one to which he or she was assigned at birth, and ultimately takes steps to present himself or herself as a person of that other sex. Transsexuals are a subset of the larger category of transgender, which can also include cross-dressers, androgynous individuals, third-gender, and those making political statements.
- Gender roles are beliefs about how men and women ought to behave; these roles vary in cultures around the world. Gender stereotypes are beliefs about what the "typical" man and woman are like. Within any category, some individuals do not fit the stereotype well, and some stereotypes reflect unfounded negative social attitudes or misinformation.

HOW DO THE SEXES DIFFER?

- All theories of human behavior emphasize that men and women are similar in most ways. Sex differences in children's play styles and toy preferences are explained differently by different researchers. Very young children have rigid ideas about appropriate play and behavior for males and females. Young infants already display sex-typed play and toy preferences. Childhood sex-typed play styles for boys include higher levels of "propulsive" behavior and rough-and-tumble play. Girls' play is characterized by less physical assertion and aggression, and more focus on interrelationships among playmates.
- Evidence exists to support two general approaches to explaining sex differences in play and toy preferences. The first stresses early social interactions and home life; for example, parents socialize their children toward sex-typical toys and play. The other approach stresses sex differences in prenatal exposure

to steroid hormones. Researchers propose that steroid hormones organize the fetal brain in ways that are expressed in infancy and childhood as play and toy preferences.

- Sex differences in cognition are controversial. Such sex differences could exist in ability, motivation, or performance. There are well-established average sex differences in performance on various cognitive tests, including tests of verbal skills, analogies, mathematics, and visual-spatial ability. However, researchers often disagree about the strength, causes, and implications of these differences.

SEXUAL BEHAVIOR: WHAT IS "HAVING SEX?"

- Although sexual behavior is one of the most important of human motivations, less is known about the psychology of sexual behavior than almost any other aspect of human life. People differ over what it means to "have sex" as a result of cultural and historical differences.
- William Masters and Virginia Johnson were the first researchers to publish detailed accounts of the physiology of human sexual response. Their sexual response cycle consisted of four phases: excitement, plateau, orgasm, and resolution. However, in their attempt to create a model that applied equally to men and women, they ignored evidence of sex differences in sexual response.

HOW DOES SEXUALITY DEVELOP?

- Although infants and children can be described as sexual beings, the sexuality of children is very different from that of adults. Human sexuality begins prior to birth, and masturbation is quite common in infancy. Sex play with peers begins in early childhood, and the majority of children probably engage in at least some sex play at some time.
- Adolescence is a particularly important point along a continuum that begins before birth. Characteristic emotional and psychological changes occur during puberty, in addition to anatomical and physiological changes.

Romantic and sexual feelings are among the most characteristic aspects of adolescence. Although it is difficult to gather reliable data, it is probably accurate that by age 18, the majority of men and women have had sexual intercourse.

WHAT IS SEXUAL ORIENTATION?

- A person's sexual orientation can be heterosexual, homosexual, or bisexual; it includes elements of behavior, desire, and identity. The three-factor model of sexual orientation is based on all three factors. The desire-driven model proposes that a person's sexual orientation is based on the sex to which the person is most strongly attracted. According to the continuum model, a person may be "slightly gay," "somewhat straight," "completely straight," and so forth.
- Patterns of sexual orientation development and expression differ for men and women. Substantially more "heterosexual" women than men report at least some sexual attraction to their own sex, and substantially more "homosexual" women than gay men report at least some attraction to the other sex. Although causes of sexual orientation are not known with certainty, researchers have identified various influencing factors, including both environmental and genetic influences.

HOW CLOSELY ARE SEX AND LOVE LINKED?

- Romantic or passionate love is a set of characteristic emotions, motivations, cognitions, and goal-directed behaviors. Romantic love is a human universal. Despite cultural differences, the quality and expressions of romantic love are more similar than different among cultures.
- Sex and love often occur together. Lisa Diamond proposed that love and sex are not always connected, because they have different evolutionary histories and are controlled by different hormones and neurotransmitters. Sex steroids estrogen and testosterone are the primary systems governing sexual desire, whereas "reward centers"

Looking Back continued

of the brain and the hormones and neurotransmitters which fluctuate within these centers—primarily dopamine, oxytocin, and the endorphins—govern affectional bonds. Love may have evolved to serve a commitment function, whereas sexual desire evolved to serve a reproductive function.

Key Terms

Affordances, 784
Anal intercourse, 798
Bisexual, 810
Clitoral hood, 801
Congenital adrenal hyperplasia (CAH), 785
Correlate, 813
Gender, 776
Gender identity, 775
Gender roles, 779
Gender schema theory, 777
Gender stereotypes, 780
Genitals, 775
Gonad, 774
Heterosexual, 810
Homosexual, 810
Hooking up, 800

Human sexual response cycle, 801
Human sexual response, 801
Human sexuality, 773
Intersex, 775
Masturbation, 806
Oral-genital sex, 798
Orgasm, 801
Orgasmic platform, 801
Ovaries, 774
Penile erection, 801
Plateau, 801
Primary sex characteristics, 806
Quantitative performance, 792
Refractory period, 801
Resolution, 801
Sadism-masochism (SM), 799
Secondary sex characteristics, 806

Serial orgasms, 802
Sex differences in cognition, 787
Sex play, 806
Sex reassignment surgery, 778
Sex-typed play and toy preferences, 782
Sexual aggression, 803
Sexual fantasy, 799
Sexual intercourse, 798
Sexual orientation, 811
Stereotype threat, 794
Testes, 774
Transgender, 778
Transsexual, 778
Vaginal lubrication, 801
Verbal performance, 791
Visual-spatial performance, 792

Test Yourself

1. What are the four determinants of sex from conception to birth?
2. From a scientific perspective, what is at least one problem with trying to separate "sex" and "gender?"
3. One's subjective perception of the sex to which one belongs or with which one identifies is known as _____. Social beliefs about appropriate behavior of men and women are known as _____. Social beliefs about the behavior of the "typical" man or woman are known as _____.
4. Distinguish the term *transsexual* from *transgender*.
5. About when does gender identity begin to form?
6. A theory of gender identity which suggests that children develop cognitive templates about their own and others' sex/gender is known as _____.
7. How do evolutionary theorists explain the fact that all human beings develop gender identity so early? In other words, what makes it so important?
8. At about what ages do sex-typed toy and play preferences begin to emerge? Which sex holds stronger preferences?
9. What sort of research evidence supports the importance of social factors in the development of sex-typed toy and play preferences? What research evidence collected among CAH girls and nonhuman mammals supports the influence of prenatal hormonal exposure?
10. Name the three areas of cognitive performance in which sex differences commonly exist.
11. Women, but not men, experience the _____ phase of the sexual response cycle. Men, but not women, experience a _____ period following orgasm.
12. Describe experiments which demonstrated differences in how men and women become aroused to erotic videotapes.
13. From her interviews with adolescent girls, Sharon Thompson describes two versions of a "same story" about first experiences of sexual initiation. Briefly characterize the differences between "Same Story A" and "Same Story B."
14. Why are figures for the average age of first intercourse for American teenagers possibly unreliable?
15. Explain the differences between desire, behavior, and identity as applied to sexual orientation. Give two possible examples of situations where these three factors could be in conflict.
16. What is meant by a "continuum model" of sexual orientation?
17. Describe at least two ways in which patterns of sexual orientation differ for men and women.
18. Describe at least three biological markers (correlates) of gay male sexual identity.